Roy A. Harrisville is Professor of New Testament at Luther Theological Seminary, St. Paul, Minnesota. Philip A. Quanbeck II is a doctoral candidate at Princeton Theological Seminary, Princeton, New Jersey.

The Influence of the
Holy Spirit

A Biblical-Theological Study
by
HERMANN GUNKEL

The Influence of the Holy Spirit

The Popular View of the Apostolic Age
and the Teaching of the Apostle Paul
translated by
ROY A. HARRISVILLE
and
PHILIP A. QUANBECK II

FORTRESS PRESS   PHILADELPHIA

BS
680
. H56
G8613

This book is a translation of *Die Wirkungen des heiligen Geistes nach der populären Anschauung der apostolischen Zeit und der Lehre des Apostels Paulus* (Göttingen: Vandenhoeck & Ruprecht, 1888).

Biblical quotations from the Revised Standard Version of the Bible, copyright 1946, 1952, © 1971, 1973 by the Division of Christian Education of the National Council of the Churches of Christ in the U.S.A., are used by permission.

Library of Congress Cataloging in Publication Data

Gunkel, Hermann, 1862–1932.
  The influence of the Holy Spirit.
  Translation of Die Wirkungen des heiligen Geistes.
  Includes index.
  1. Holy Spirit—Biblical teaching. I. Title.
BS680.H56C8613   231'.3   78-20022
ISBN 0-8006-0544-6

7417L78   Printed in the United States of America   1–544

CONTENTS

Introduction

by ROY A. HARRISVILLE

The name Hermann Gunkel is as familiar to biblical scholars as their own. Gunkel founded a "school," fathered form-critical research, and taught most of the giants of the last generation, and his literary efforts constitute the greater part of that volcanic productivity in biblical studies of the last century which contemporary scholars spend much of their time struggling to comprehend. His *Einleitung in die Psalmen,* for example, still has the floor in the debate concerning the Bible's poetic literature.

Here is what at first sight appears to be a modest little work by the "early Gunkel"; indeed, it is the very first to come from his pen. Matched against the activity of the established thinker, the piece seems elementary, perhaps even clumsy (see Gunkel's own appraisal in the Preface).

The method of the more mature genius is, of course, recognizable. Gunkel refuses the task of interpretation without thought for the history and traditions of Jew, Hellene, and Hellenist. The difference may be the delight, even awe, with which the younger, struggling scholar here makes discoveries.

The prejudices and presuppositions of the more mature Gunkel, those things he shared with all his tribe and for which he is no longer celebrated, are also present in this little work, though in initial form: the fixing of the gospel's uniqueness—once parallels in extrabiblical thought have torn away the theory of an originality of ideas—in "religion" or "experience"; the daubing of "doctrine" with a big, black brush, and the concomitant notion that creativity in Israel ended with the major prophets, that the religion of the Spirit, in the words of another contemporary, had become the religion of a book; the resultant sanguine but so fragile assumption that recovery of the historical Jesus would save Christianity from a similar fate; the anxiety in face of the Bible's use of imagination, and a nod in the direction of that bloodless accenting of "what does it mean?" later come to meet us in the form of a demythologizing program; and finally, the hermeneutical requirement of "imitation" (*nachempfinden, nacherleben,* and *nachfühlen*) for a true interpretation. What came to be the exposed and unprotected flank of an entire generation of scholars is turned to the reader here.

But despite the youth and vulnerability of its author at the time of its writing, this little book is still the round, smooth stone that felled a Goliath who had dared any to come against him since Hegel and the Enlightenment. That swollen, preening Philistine was the notion that "Spirit," and the "Spirit" of the Bible above all (since it represented an "advance" in rational religion), was the equivalent of human consciousness. Gunkel believed the Goliath would not have appeared had there been no attempt to recognize Spirit as an objectively present entity. The reason lay deeper—in the assumption that the divine was disclosed to consciousness since consciousness, whose other name is "Spirit," was of the essence of the human *and* the divine, and that thus one merely needed a good head (enter objectivity) by which to discern the ways of God with men. No matter what the reason, armed with what from current perspective can only be called rough tools, Gunkel put an end to, or, at least, for anyone who can read he put an end to, that vast notion. "Spirit," wrote Gunkel, is not the principle of the religious-moral life—the first critical step toward the identification of Spirit with human consciousness—for what Spirit does cannot be identified through intelligibility. On the contrary, Spirit spells the irrational, the inexplicable; it marks what cannot be grasped by an effort of the mind—it is supernatural. There is thus no "purpose" to Spirit, said Gunkel, enabling one to read off the divine origin of a deed from its value to an individual or community. Indeed, in the most primitive period, "Spirit" is either good or evil. And as to its nature, far from suggesting incorporeality, those terms *wind* and *breath* are calculated to conjure up thoughts of substance, of air, or light or fire. As for Paul, the great speculator, he agreed with the primitive notion, saw the Spirit in ecstatic gibberish, in mantic prophecy, in a transcendent invasion of the person never to be identified with the "I"—but with one proviso. Paul insisted that the "gifts" of the Spirit be used for edification, that their exercise was of ethical significance. For this reason the apostle came to describe the entirety of Christian existence as pneumatic. Lest his reader find in this last result some occasion for the emergence of that old Goliath, Gunkel concluded that the evidence demonstrated that Paul's insistence upon the gifts as used for the common good was not a judgment from experience but a quite arbitrary constraint of love placed on the pneumatic. Edification, then, did not constitute the mark of the Spirit's gift; again, or still, it was the irrational, the inexplicable, the "not-I."

Against what he had found with respect to "Spirit" Gunkel measured everything else—Messiah, faith, freedom, flesh, and kingdom. Indeed, he had one stone left for any who believed "kingdom" marked some brotherhood of man realizable by human effort. "Every kingdom exists so long as there is a power to preserve it," he wrote, and on the basis of the evidence he contended that the power which supports that order of things in which the divine will is manifest is transcendent, that is, "it is present wherever the Spirit of God enters to break the devil's might." Whatever other stones were left in Gunkel's bag we leave the reader to discover.

It was his concession to personality, to the individual as vehicle or bearer of transcendence, which made it difficult for Gunkel to allow to the New Testament authors, particularly to Paul, any thought of Spirit which did not root in experience. He went so far as to insist that what could not be traced to the religious life had no value, a tenet bequeathed to a subsequent generation for which the term *existential* would carry so much freight. For this reason, the relation between Paul's teaching concerning the Spirit and his teaching concerning Christ remained something of an enigma to Gunkel. He was aware of Paul's preference for the latter, and of the former as rooted in the apostle's education and experiences with his churches, and he concluded that the teaching about Christ was the peculiarly Pauline expression of what the apostle was contending for in his doctrine of the Spirit. Gunkel could even write that the apostle's teaching regarding the Spirit took on its peculiar shape from his conversion. But these remain merely hints or clues at best, and their context is still that concession to experience, the experience of the religious personality. Where the two strains come together is the point where Paul's experience constitutes a reflection or refraction—what God had accomplished in Jesus Christ "while we were enemies," before belief, before experience, before conversion.

Still, David was not the only shepherd boy in Israel, merely the greatest, and Gunkel was not the only giant-killer, though his hope that this little book would soon be outdated by an "abundance of new discoveries" has still not been fulfilled, at least not altogether. Even if he had not killed Goliath, the killing of the lion or the bear would have been reason enough for telling his story. Who remembers J. Gloël, or who ranks Wendt and Pfleiderer with Gunkel? Those were the lions and the bears. But Gunkel did kill Goliath, and this little piece is his Valley of Elah.

Just now, when reaction to formalistic religion requires that every Christian person exercise such unusual gifts as Holy Writ describes, it is necessary to remember that such a reaction is but the obverse side of that coin of the identification of Spirit with consciousness—one great giant of a notion felled long years ago, by Hermann Gunkel, in 1888.

Author's Preface to the Second and Third German Editions[1]

The present publication, the author's first, initially appeared in 1888 and has found unexpected favorable reception with the theological public, especially in recent years. The publisher informs me that the book, which has for some time been out of print, is continually requested, and it has been decided to publish it again. Faced with the question as to whether and to what extent I wished to make changes in the new printing, I have let various considerations induce me to leave the book unchanged. For though I still hold to the basic position set forth in it, a fresh treatment of the same theme would mean an altogether new book. But I will not write this new book, not now, when I am occupied by other literary activities, nor later. I must content myself with having furnished a stimulus in the area. But I use this occasion to indicate briefly what kind of new treatment I have in mind, and also to refer to Heinrich Weinel's *Die Wirkungen des Geistes und der Geister im nachapostolischen Zeitalter* (1899). In this excellent book I recognize the legitimate continuation of my studies and observe with particular delight that in going beyond the results I then obtained, Weinel has advanced to views and methods that were also disclosed to me throughout the years.[2]

1. This preface, prefixed to the second edition, has been examined for the third edition, but I have refrained from essentially altering the words written in 1899, and wish to be understood from that date.

2. From the literature which has since appeared, and which I no longer have been able to pursue completely, I refer especially to Wilhelm Bousset's very worthwhile and in turn forward-leading review of Weinel's work in the "Göttinger Gelehrte Anzeige," 1901, pp. 753ff. [Addition to the third edition.]

The real task of my little work was to ascertain the symptoms by which an "effect" of the Spirit was recognized, and in face of the modernizings of exegetes who, without historical reflection and influenced by rationalism, know nothing of the "effects" of the πνεῦμα and render "Spirit" a pure abstraction. It was thus my concern not to describe individual pneumatic phenomena but to set forth what was common to them all and thus the typically pneumatic. I had also realized that the task first of all is not to produce a New Testament doctrine of the Spirit but rather to describe the specific experience of the pneumatic.

Now, however, the goal of any further treatment of this theme would have to be a graphic presentation of individual effects of the Spirit in the apostolic age, and on the basis of these findings. For this there is abundant and extremely significant material available, by which a host of unintelligible or half-understood passages can take on new light—as Weinel has already demonstrated for a large part of the New Testament and often in such a surprising and happy way. It would be particularly fruitful to investigate the pneumatic aspect in the person of the Lord. Actually, my book dealt with many pneumatic experiences, but of course not in total or in sufficient depth. This was due in part to the limited character of the theme as sketched above. Moreover, I was hindered by the then prevailing situation, which posed all but insurmountable difficulties for such an academic research. After all, in those days every future researcher had first to win by his own sweat the foundations of a truly historical exegesis of the New Testament. Being at that time a young, unproven beginner, and faced with many a contradiction, I was forced on every hand to state clearly and to defend the position I had just won (for this reason I hope the present reader will excuse the book's frequent polemic) and had neither time nor energy to deepen it sufficiently. When I reexamine my work now, I am struck above all by the fact that it often describes the pneumatic phenomena from the standpoint of an alien, aloof observer. It would be wiser and more appropriate first of all to interpret those phenomena just as the pneumatic himself perceived them. But this divergence of my present opinion from my opinion at that time is no accident. The latter suited the level of my development at which I could very well regard these mysterious appearances, so removed from common sense, as an alien observer, but clearly could not be sympathetic to them as if they were my own. Now I believe I have a better and more discerning knowledge of the subject, particularly from a more thorough reading of the Old Testament prophets, and I see that these things take on life—though but from a distance—only when we are able to live the pneumatic's inner states after him. At that time, I believed that the conviction that a person has a spirit or demon results from certain perceptions formed by the alien observer. Since he cannot explain certain phenomena in any other way he interprets them as the effect of some supernatural being. Now I see that the conviction that a spirit is speaking or acting through the pneumatic is not a later conclusion drawn by another but the direct experience of the one inspired. In this manner one senses those experiences as the effects of an alien being, of a power not the "I," and wishing to dissuade the one who has had them from this conviction would be as useless as a blind person's insisting to someone who can see that there is no sun at all because he himself does not see it. Thus, whoever happens to write on this theme in the future, or otherwise intends to form an independent judgment on it, must first somehow put himself in a position to share the feeling of the pneumatic. In any event, he should trust not me or others like me but the prophets of the Old and the pneumatics of the New Testament, that genuine, psychological events are at issue here, not phrases or superstition. Though imitation and dogma may play a great role in this area as well, though even superstition may be close at hand, none of it would exist if real events were not underlying.

Whoever intends to describe such pneumatic experiences may not, for instance, describe only New Testament matters. The material in the New Testament is too meager for that and too difficult to interpret, just as the earlier and quite self-evident isolation of the New Testament in scientific investigation variously hindered a truly vital grasp of the history of New Testament religion. In the present work the author has at least added the Old Testament and Judaism. The fact that the latter was mishandled was novel to this special area eleven years ago. Then, even in a biblical theology of the New Testament, Judaism was as good as totally ignored by many researchers, and where New Testament doctrines were concerned, it was deemed scientific to search the Old Testament for "points of contact," as the *technicus terminus* read. Today the situation has been greatly altered, but there is still much to do until we gain an intimate knowledge of the religious life of Judaism. But even with this added dimension, the material would not yet be sufficient but would leave the quite improper impression that such phenomena occurred only in Israel. Of course, the organized church of every age maintains that the epoch of the prophets and of revelation is past. In reality, however, the pneumatic phenomena have merely retreated, have never died out. They reappear in the light of history in special times and persons and are present even among us. I am thinking merely of the history of mysticism or of occultism. And these events occur not merely in the Christian church. There is scarcely a folk or a religion where similar phenomena could not be found. So there is a vast, almost incalculable, and extremely multiform material that must all the more be set in motion in order to understand the New Testament phenomena. We should not be afraid that this will obscure the originality of the New Testament pneumatic phenomena or of the great bearers of the Spirit throughout history. It will not obscure this, only illumine it. All the history of religion, when pursued in a suitably comprehensive and wise fashion, will serve only to demonstrate the originality and marvelous grandeur of primitive Christianity, particularly of the gospel.

In the present little work this material outside the New Testament is given too short shrift. When I first wrote this book the prophets were scarcely known to me from every aspect, and, as far as I know, there was no theological publication from which I could have learned to understand their pneumatic experiences. Now, as then, a description of "prophetism" which really laid hold of the matter is still lacking. What has been written on this theme serves the dogmatic aim of interpreting the prophetic experiences from the perspective of a given author's world view much more than it does the historical purpose of describing and conceiving them psychologically. What depressed me then with regard to Judaism was the still-universal prejudice that there were no pneumatic experiences at all in that period.[3] Further, a deeper

---

3. For the moment, see, e.g., my statements regarding the visionary experiences of the "prophet Ezra" in *Apokryphen und Pseudepigraphen des Alten Testaments,* ed. Emil F. Kautzsch (Tübingen, n.d.), vol. 2. [Addition to the third edition.]

penetration of the topic was made more difficult by the tendency to pursue the term πνεῦμα when describing the religious phenomenon of the πνεῦμα, a tendency which clings to much of the research on "biblical-theological concepts" like a chronic disease and which I well knew even then to be a fundamental error—whoever hangs on the term cannot see the life—but from which I was still not able to keep myself totally free.

At that time I lacked material for church history, for what is contemporary, and for other religions. All in all, I lacked a view that was able to embrace the individual detail. Further, I was not totally unaware that certain nervous states are related to pneumatic phenomena, or at times match them more or less closely. In our texts, insanity and possession by the Spirit are in fact often compared. In the Old Testament both are denoted by the same term: התנבא. But here too the material was not at my disposal. A future reviser would have to make up for all this. Weinel, whose book I have cited above, is already master of material greater by far than I was then.[4]

In order to evaluate pneumatic experiences we must first of all sharply distinguish the experience of the pneumatic himself from the interpretation given it by him or his observers. Such interpretation varies according to the cultural epoch and religion of the evaluator. In instances in which we today see nothing but nervousness, illness, or insanity—I am thinking of Saul's melancholy or of the demonic in Jesus' day—the ancient period thought to find supernatural causes. But even interpretation can diverge most widely, according to the various religious epochs. The Israelite prophet of the older period sensed the impact of Yahweh in his ecstasies and visions; the prophets of the later period dared only think of an angel in such an instance. What they sensed was at bottom the same, or at least something very similar—only the interpretation they gave the experience was different. In ancient Israel, where nationality and religion interpenetrated and where ancient naiveté did not yet recognize the distinction between the secular and the sacred which dominated the later period, influences of God's Spirit were seen even in certain

4. In a manner most deserving of thanks, Bousset refers to further material in the "Göttinger Gelehrte Anzeige," 1901, pp. 762ff. [Addition to the third edition.]

experiences that a later age would have marked down as profane. Thus in antiquity the wondrous power of the artist, the uncanny wisdom of the judge, and the superhuman bravery of the hero were derived from Yahweh. In the most primitive period, one had no compunctions about encountering Yahweh's Spirit even in the lusty brawler Samson, or of conceiving an insane person as possessed by the Spirit "from Yahweh." No wonder, then, that in the New Testament age the symptoms of demons and the Spirit are so alike—originally, the demonic as well belongs to men of the Spirit. The remarkable parallel in Paul's utterances concerning the Spirit and concerning oneness with Christ is to be understood in this light. Two separate interpretations of the same experience are involved. The experiences are to be interpreted from out of Paul's person, and the two series of interpretations which he gives them from out of the history of religion.

I will add here a few observations on the history of religions. When an ancient—and on occasion even a later—period refers to many spirits, this is not a later differentiation of the one Spirit of Yahweh but rather the most primitive idea, older even than the religion of Yahweh itself, an idea stoutly thrust into the background by the Yahweh religion but not entirely eliminated. In the New Testament age, this primeval polydemonism appears again in the form of belief in all sorts of demons. It makes its appearance in another sphere, in the Testaments of the Twelve Patriarchs. When this writing derives every human deed, resolution, and thought, indeed, even the seven senses from good or evil spirits, these are not the author's "fantasies"; but they are very interesting—though judged from a religious point of view quite worthless—vestiges of primeval religion.[5] Finally, it is appropriate to note here that despite the assertion of church dogma the Spirit has never really become a person in the faith of humankind. Since time immemorial, something indeterminate, impalpable, and impersonal has clung to the idea of Spirit, and ex-

5. For the moment, see the extensive literature compiled by Carl Brockelmann in *Zeitschrift für alttestamentliche Wissenschaft* (Tübingen, 1906), p. 31. In addition, see Bernhard Stade, *Biblische Theologie des Alten Testaments*, 1:140, and Wilhelm Heitmüller, *Im Namen Jesu* (Göttingen: Vandenhoeck & Ruprecht, 1903), p. 165. [Addition to the third edition.]

6

periences in which one sensed the impact of a person have instead been assigned to Yahweh, to an angel, or to Christ.

In addition, it is necessary for the historian of religion to recognize the great variety in individual pneumatic experiences and do them justice. Pneumatic impulses of will—I am using the language of Weinel—can involve, for example, a quite aimless raving, running, and leaping but also the highest and most noble stirrings of the will of which mankind is capable, and both can meet in the same person. For this reason, findings with respect to the pneumatic may be of no value at all for the great history of religion—in ancient Israel the seer occasionally answered questions regarding the whereabouts of stray cattle—but on the other hand the greatest persons to whom we owe everything were pneumatic. The historian, however, should have eyes for the whole.

Accordingly, the evaluation of pneumatic experiences for the history of religion must be made with great care. Everywhere churches have canonized the pneumatics of a given past, and, where possible, they have relegated those of their own time to the periphery as heretics and fanatics. Protestant churches in particular, with their sole veneration of *scriptura sacra,* have not allowed a modern pneumatic to emerge who might have been a threat to this authority. Even the Enlightenment found only superstition and fanaticism here. In the joy of first discovery, a modern trend in the other direction is in danger of vastly overestimating these things. But this danger of one-sidedness on the one or other hand is emphatically to be avoided. The historian, cognizant of a great amount of material, will certainly not prize such phenomena as such. Often enough, they are scarcely distinguishable from illness, and their content, religiously speaking, is frequently of the most worthless kind. In some instances, however, the historian will defer to them in awe and wonder, since he knows that the epoch-making religious experiences have almost always appeared in this form, that the decisive religious personalities were for the most part pneumatic, and that the greatest epochs in religion were often pneumatic. But here too the historian will guard against exaggeration—πνεῦμα and religion are not identical. We hear nothing of the πνεῦμα in the great and fundamental ideas of the Sermon on the Mount, and certainly Paul Gerhardt was no pneumatic.

Pneumatic experiences are to be differentiated sharply from the doctrine of or speculation on the Spirit, where complex religious-historical constructs may be involved. Even Paul's speculation regarding the Spirit poses a very difficult problem. As clear to us as Paul's own perception is, together with the experiences which form its background (this is set forth in the present work), just as difficult is it for us to recognize the history that accounts for the interpretations he found and the further ideas he attached to them. I can no longer believe that this speculation is to be understood solely from Paul's experiences. The fact that the language of this speculation already appears in fully fixed form speaks against it. His utterances concerning oneness with Christ pose an even more difficult historical problem. Here too language teaches us to assume a prior history. But since I am not in a position now to describe this problem in detail, I will forego even hinting at a possible solution here and shall be content merely to make reference to these questions.

It is very likely that the time for composing a complete history of the πνεῦμα has not yet arrived. In the meantime, it must be a matter of monographs. The model for such treatment is Weinel's work mentioned above, which has as its theme the period from Paul to Irenaeus. I hope that the other epochs of history will soon claim the attention of scholars; that the early apostolic period and Paul, to the extent not yet covered by Weinel, will not on that account be forgotten; and that the present little book will soon be totally outdated by an abundance of new discoveries.

Introduction

In the history of primitive Christianity the activities of the Spirit are a factor of greatest significance. They assumed widest scope in the life of the earliest communities, as the Book of Acts and the Pauline Epistles both make clear. We may justly assert that, alongside other factors, earliest Christianity retained its peculiar character, perceptible in all its varying tendencies, not least from the conviction that it had the Spirit. For Paul too our contention is no doubt correct. Within his world of ideas as well the Spirit is a most important and unique concept. For this reason biblical-theological scholarship has been occupied with Paul's teaching concerning the Spirit. But there has been much less discussion of the views which the oldest community prior to and in addition to Paul entertained of the Spirit and his activities. Even in the most recent publication,[1] which gives detailed analysis of Paul's teaching concerning the πνεῦμα, the ideas of the communities regarding the Spirit are scarcely taken into account—at a disadvantage to the subject. For it cannot be disputed that even Paul's position at this point in his teaching can be properly understood and evaluated only when we first consider the ideas that were available to the apostle within Christian circles.

In what follows, the question will be raised as to what type of phenomena the communities and Paul regarded as pneumatic, and why it is these that are derived from the Spirit. This will enable us to define the concept of an activity of the Spirit and thus that of the Spirit himself, and will help us to show the relation between the Spirit and similar concepts. We can do this, of course, only if we continually

---

1. J. Gloël, *Der heilige Geist in der Heilsverkündigung des Paulus* (Halle, 1888).

keep in mind the significance of the Spirit for the Christian life. By taking this path toward the concept of "Spirit" and thus often exceeding the limits of biblical theology, we hope to present a livelier picture of the πνεῦμα than if we were to occupy ourselves merely with the dogmatic concept of "Spirit."

1.
The Popular Views

THE MATTER OF SOURCES

What are the sources in which we can recognize how the primitive Christian community viewed the Spirit and his activities? In the letters of Paul himself, especially in 1 Corinthians, we find a series of statements in which Paul refers to popular views held in the community. Here then are ideas as they existed in Gentile Christian churches. Most recent scholars often assert that the view of the divine Spirit and his activities which must have been held at Corinth is to be explained by the influence of originally pagan religious ideas.[1] For this reason we must examine other sources in order to test the Christian character of the Corinthian views.

The ideas of the earliest Jewish-Christian community are found in the synoptic Gospels and their sources. Among them, Luke, of course, is to be used with caution because he is in part dependent on Paul. The most important source, and for us the most comprehensive by far, is the Book of Acts. Naturally, what was said of the third Gospel applies to this source as well. In addition to possible Pauline influence, we must observe whether or not it betrays the perspective of a later generation. But, as none will deny, Acts still rests on older, and for our task exceptionally rich, sources, which, of course, can seldom be peeled away with any certainty. Next, the Apocalypse—even in the event it should be a "Christian revision of a Jewish exemplar"—is at

---

1. C.F.W. v. Weizsäcker, *Das apostolische Zeitalter* (Freiburg im Breisgau, 1888), p. 298; C.F. Georg Heinrici, *Das erste Sendschreiben des Apostels Paulus an die Korinther* (Berlin, 1880), p. 390.

least to be used in its clearly Christian orientation and sup-plementation.

We may use other writings of the New Testament—there is no agreement as yet regarding their independence from or dependence on Paul—only when we find in them parallels to such sequences of ideas as have already been recognized as early apostolic (1 Peter, James, and the Gospel and Epistles of John). The same method applies to the Deutero-Pauline literature (Ephesians, Hebrews, the Pastorals, and perhaps 2 Thessalonians).

We will not err if in our evaluation of the above-named sources we continually keep to what is common and consistent in the primitive Christian view but on the other hand proceed with special caution where the individual sources diverge or are not harmonious.

Since we will be making our way in part on uncertain ground, the question as to what kinds of sources this portion of our research will use for corroborating, clarifying, and throwing light on the results obtained is of special significance. On the occasion of a similar theme, H. H. Wendt[2] has set up a method of "examining Paul's utterances to determine whether or not they can be explained from Old Testament usage." This method, which Wendt seeks to apply even to the majority of the remaining New Testament authors, is—apart from his polemic against interpreting Paul on the basis of Hellenistic ideas— not quite correct.

Wendt does not consider a factor of primary importance among pre-Christian assumptions with respect to the usage and sphere of ideas in the apostolic age: Judaism. In Emil Schürer's judgment, the legal orientation dominated all religious life in the time of Christ. "Thus," Schürer writes, "in that period even the Old Testament with the great abundance of its religious ideas edged toward the in-dividual's consciousness only by the light given it from legalistic Judaism."[3] Now, of course, the preaching of Jesus is altogether congenial to prophetism. The gospel possessed by the earliest com-munity is a fresh sprout from the old, all-but-withered root of Old

---

2. H.H. Wendt, *Die Begriffe Fleisch und Geist* (Gotha, 1878), p. 90.

3. Emil Schürer, *Die Predigt Jesu in ihrem Verhältnis zum Alten Testament und zum Judentum* (Darmstadt, 1882), p. 5.

Testament prophecy. And the gospel did not emerge or spread without Old Testament influence. But it is certain that we must proceed with greatest care if we intend to demonstrate New Testament views as the effects of Old Testament ideas that had died out in Judaism. First of all, the assumption of Jewish influence always carries much greater probability than does the assumption of the influence of the Old Testament. And in any case, it is an error of great magnitude to ignore Judaism as such. We must therefore designate Judaism as the real matrix of the gospel—the apostles emerged from Jewish ideas, and with Jewish ideas they had to come to terms with one another—but without denying the influence of a reading of the Old Testament. In each individual instance it is the task of biblical theology to arrive at a decision concerning the origin of a New Testament idea—a task that has indeed been conceded but not yet really taken up. But the only type of Judaism we shall consider in this first chapter (the purpose of which is to develop the views of the primitive Christian community) is Palestinian Judaism. For many questions the application of this method is of greatest significance, and though it is not unimportant where our questions are concerned, it is still not really essential, for in the matter of the Spirit's activities we have to do with an ancient Hebrew or perhaps primitive Semitic conception that had undergone only slight changes in the apostolic age. Further, the Old Testament sources yield a richer material by far. But even in this instance, the use of Jewish literature alongside the Old Testament is a matter of course.

AN EARLY APOSTOLIC DOCTRINE
OF THE SPIRIT?

Our most important observation, one which is decisive for grasping what was understood by "Holy Spirit" in the apostolic period, is that the primitive community was not at all concerned with a doctrine of the Holy Spirit and his activities.[4] What is involved here is not a creedal statement, as was, for example, the assertion of Jesus' resurrection for those who had not seen and yet believed. Rather, at issue are quite concrete facts, obvious to all, which were the object of

4. Contra Otto Pfleiderer, *Paulinismus* (Leipzig, 1873), p. 202, who says of the "traditional doctrine" that "the πνεῦμα is received in baptism."

daily experience and without further reflection were directly experienced as effected by the Spirit. In the eyes of the primitive Christian community these manifestations render the presence of the Spirit an undeniable fact. So it is conceivable that apart from the allusions of a person such as Paul, a man by nature given to reflection, we find in our sources absolutely no doctrinal statements regarding the Spirit, though we find a host of descriptions of the Spirit's activities. We who live in a later age and do not as a matter of course have analogous experiences on which to draw can only grasp the primitive, apostolic view of the Spirit by proceeding from his activities as reported to us and by attempting to conceive the Spirit as the power calling forth these activities.

The same holds true of the Old Testament. It is a dangerous error[5] to conceive the Spirit in the Old Testament—to the extent that genuine religious and moral activities do not fall to his share—as "on the whole" belonging "to an antiquity adorned by legend" or to an "ideal end time," and thus to assign his activities "on the whole" to fantasy and not to real history. If the notion of Spirit in ancient Israel had not been uncommonly vivid, a fact that can often enough be proved with examples, then its origin and persistence throughout many centuries up to the apostolic age would be totally inconceivable. Moreover, pneumatic personalities are named in whom the Spirit worked nothing principally religious or moral—we refer, for example, to Saul—and we must reckon with the fact that because of the great gaps in the description of the history of Israel handed down to us, we are almost always dependent on inferences from the nonhistorical books for a description of popular life in Israel.

Indeed, in the sources of the New Testament which we cited above, as well as in Judaism and the Old Testament, the most varied activity is conceived as belonging to the Spirit.[6] It is all the more necessary to treat in detail the question concerning what was common to all these spiritual phenomena. But since we are dealing here with an idea that was unusually vital in primitive Christianity, we may not hold to

5. Wendt, *Begriffe,* p. 35.
6. Enumerations are offered in ibid., pp. 32ff.; Eduard Reuss, *Geschichte des Alten Testaments* (Braunschweig, 1881), p. 317; Hermann Schultz, *Alttestamentliche Theologie,* 2d ed. (Frankfurt am Main, 1878), p. 545.

theorems that a later historiographer (Luke) or dogmatician (Paul) may offer but must set ourselves in the apostolic period and ask, What were the symptoms by which earliest Christianity determined that a phenomenon was an activity of the Spirit?

THE SPIRIT AT WORK ON AND THROUGH THE PERSON

We must note first that not "all self-attestation and activity of God, or the revelation in its entire compass" is traced to the Spirit.[7] Rather, only a portion of all those events in which the divine intervenes in earthly life is regarded as an activity of the Spirit. Almost without exception, only those events that impinge on human existence are described as activities of the Spirit. Thus, the ἐνεργήματα τοῦ πνεύματος never involve the effects of God on nature but always involve activities toward the person, pertaining solely to his inner life or enabling him to appear as actor in certain mighty deeds of the Spirit. The Spirit works on and through the person. Thus, such divine activities as an earthquake, or such an event in the Old Testament as the destruction of a city, or divine blessings in nature, and so on are not derived from the Spirit of God. On the other hand, in the New Testament all activities of the Spirit can be derived from God or Christ, and almost all from an angel. An exception to the first rule appears in 2 Kings 2:14, 15, in which the Spirit of Yahweh divides the water of the Jordan in order to prove by an external, natural occurrence that the Spirit, with his wondrous power, has passed from Elijah to Elisha. A bit more enigmatic is the "spirit of judgment and . . . spirit of burning" in Isa. 4:4, by which Yahweh will cleanse the iniquities of Jerusalem. It is possible that the prophet has in mind that Yahweh will raise up men who by this Spirit will purge the wicked from the earth (Isa. 11:4). But it is also possible that he conceives the spirit of judgment and destruction as a devastating, divine storm which snatches the godless from Israel's midst (such as, e.g., in Isa. 30:28; 40:7; Job 4:9; 15:30; Wisd. of Sol. 5:23; 11:20; see 2 Thess. 2:8). In the latter case, we would note a second exception to the rule.

7. Contra Hermann Cremer, *Wörterbuch der neutestamentlichen Gräcität*, 5th ed. (Gotha, 1888), p. 741.

The New Testament might furnish such exception in the idea underlying the infancy narrative in Luke and in Matthew, according to
which Jesus was conceived by the Holy Spirit—which is intended to
mean that for Jesus, and not as for ordinary persons chosen by God to
be prophets, the Holy Spirit was not something added to nature, a
donum superadditum, but rather the agent who continually and
totally filled his life, just as it was the Spirit who began it. This
thought is conveyed by the idea of the Spirit of God as a creative spirit
of life, an idea usually separated from that of the Spirit as a principle
of divine activities in and through the person.

THE SPIRIT AND THE
MORAL-RELIGIOUS SPHERE

It is a well-known observation that according to the popular view[8]
the Spirit is not, as it is for Paul, the principle of the Christian
religious-moral life and that the Spirit is thus not regarded as author
of all Christian action. And when J. E. Gloël[9] supposes that in Acts
the total "religious and moral life of fellowship in the earliest community" is an effect of the Spirit, this can be proved neither from the
Pentecost narrative, in which the Spirit directly works only glossolalia
and prophecy, nor from Acts 2:42–47, in which there is not one
syllable to indicate that the ideal state of the community described
derives from the Spirit. In Acts 4:31 that which is worked by the Spirit
is the courage of faith persisting in persecutions, not the consensus of
believers as reported at the beginning of a new section (Acts 4:32).[10]
But conversely, not all the Spirit's gifts of grace belong to the sphere
of the religious-moral life. Hermann Schultz's statement[11] regarding
the Old Testament, to the effect that a moral element does not directly
inhere in the word *spirit,* can be immediately applied here when, for

---

8. See Bernhard Weiss, *Lehrbuch der biblischen Theologie des Neuen Testaments,* 4th
ed. (Berlin, 1884), p. 60, n. 2; p. 129, n. 1; p. 595; Otto Pfleiderer, *Urchristentum*
(Berlin, 1887), p. 255; idem, *Paulinismus,* pp. 20, 199, 203. In recent years, Adolf von
Harnack has made a similar observation in *Lehrbuch der Dogmengeschichte,* 2d ed.
(Freiburg im Breisgau, 1888), 1:47, n. 1.
9. Gloël, *Der heilige Geist,* pp. 239–40.
10. On the passages in 6:5 and 11:24, further cited by Gloël, ibid., see below.
11. Schultz, *Alttestamentliche Theologie,* p. 547.

example, we simply recall the prophecy of a great famine which is traced to the Spirit (Acts 11:28). Thus we have the right to ask this question: In the primitive Christian community are moral or religious functions derived from the Spirit?

First of all, what is the relation of the Spirit to faith? For Acts it is a commonplace that to be a believer and to be seized by the Spirit are separate events. Only the believer, of course, can receive the Spirit, but whoever has faith does not on that account already have the Spirit (see esp. Acts 8:12–17). Faith comes through preaching, and the Spirit descends usually by the laying on of hands following baptism (Acts 8:17; 19:6) or by the laying on of hands prior to (Acts 9:17) and during baptism (Acts 2:38). The reception of the Spirit is thus God's witness to the existence of faith (Acts 15:8ff.; 11:17). Faith, then, is not derived from the Spirit but is held to be the prerequisite for receiving the Spirit. Even the first disciples—this is the view of Acts—had long been believers, even in Jesus' lifetime, and had the appearances of the risen Lord already behind them when they first shared the outpouring of the Spirit. The Gospel of John concurs with Acts in this historical perspective (John 7:39). And Jesus himself first received the Spirit in baptism!

Indeed, the Pauline utterances do not support those in Acts at all points. Paul knows nothing of a laying on of hands regularly performed (see Gal. 3:2). And in 1 Cor. 1:14 he excludes the notion that only certain persons, as in Acts, are able to convey the Spirit. We must view that custom (in the Old Testament, Deut. 34:9, etc.), still reflected in Heb. 6:2 (see 1 Tim. 4:14; 2 Tim. 1:6) and corresponding to the Jewish custom of סמיכה at the ordination of חכמים,[12] as a later institution. But Paul also confirms that the granting of the Spirit follows faith (see Gal. 4:6).

On the other hand, in such passages as Acts 6:5 and 11:24, faith and Spirit are intimately connected, and in others, such as 9:31 and 13:52, a joyful and robust persistence in faith is described as an act of the Spirit. The first two passages deal with a special energy of faith which belongs only to especially favored people, just as 9:31 and 13:52 refer

---

12. See Ferdinand Weber, *System der altsynagogalen palästinensischen Theologie* (Leipzig, 1880), pp. 123, 130, 186.

to a particular perseverance in faith, that is, a faith under persecution. It is this faith to which Paul refers when he lists πίστις in 1 Cor. 12:9 and 13:2 as one among other gifts and when he assumes that prophecy is given only to the person whose faith is especially strong and powerful (Rom. 12:6). Now, since such a view does not exactly correspond with Paul's teaching regarding faith, the apostle must have encountered it in the primitive Christian community and appropriated it. In precisely the same way, Acts 6:3,10 links to the Spirit the great wisdom of some members of the Jerusalem congregation, Stephen among them. It is a wisdom that distinguishes them from other Christians (6:3) and that no one can resist (6:10). The Pauline counterpart is the λόγος σοφίας given only to certain Christians in 1 Cor. 12:8, whose activity is quite analogously described in 2 Cor. 10:5.

When Acts 10:46 recognizes that Cornelius and his house possess the Spirit by the fact that they speak in tongues and extol God, then a μεγαλύνειν τὸν θεόν, which is pneumatic in character, is not the usual praise that any Christian may give at any time but an ecstatic praise connected with glossolalia (as ψάλλειν τῷ πνεύματι in 1 Cor. 14:15; see Acts 2:11). In this way Paul also distinguishes pneumatic prayer from ordinary prayer (1 Cor. 14:15).

We may not state, therefore, that the activities of the Spirit are indifferent to the moral-religious sphere. There are spiritual revelations that occur in this area. But the everyday religious acts of the ordinary Christian are not perceived as gifts of the Holy Spirit. Where the moral and religious aspects are regarded as pneumatic, there is always a heightening of the commonplace. Incidentally, when we speak of the Spirit we are thinking less of these activities than of prophecy, glossolalia, and so on, which do not directly pertain to the area under discussion. Zechariah and Elizabeth are not Spirit-bearers, though "walking in all the commandments and ordinances of the Lord blameless" (Luke 1:6). Simeon's "walking" does not differ from theirs—he is "righteous and devout," just as they are (Luke 2:25). And yet the Holy Spirit rests upon him—he was a prophet. If in the circle of the first Christians the Spirit was regarded first of all as the author of particularly outstanding deeds of faith and life, then Simon, the magician of Acts 8:18, would certainly not have gotten the notion of wanting to buy from the apostles the power to transmit the

Spirit. The gift of God which he wanted to buy and, of course, to exploit for profit, was something quite different. Indeed, for faith and love he would have given little money, but as the ancient or modern age teaches, the gift of prophecy, for example, can be used most profitably.[13] In Luke 1:15 a child in the womb is said to have the Spirit, and of course it can scarcely be ignored that its leaping for joy (1:44)—a homage paid the yet unborn Messiah—is conceived as an activity of the Spirit. When, in the view of an ancient period, even a βρέφος can be credited with the Spirit—and here we surely have before us a Jewish-Christian source, written before A.D. 70—then we see clearly how little of piety and morality must have inhered in the pervasive manifestations of the Spirit.

This observation is the less surprising, since it is confirmed by the Old Testament and by Judaism. The ordinary conduct of the individual, Israelite or Jew, is not derived from the Spirit. Piety and morality as such are thus not regarded as pneumatic. It is not the life that is pleasing to God but rather the instruction in it—in the prophets or in the Law—which God has given through his Spirit (see, e.g., Neh. 9:20). And even where believers are aware they have received power from God for a moral life, there is no reference to the Spirit. With the exception of Isa. 11:1,2, 28:6, 32:15ff., Ezek. 36:27 (perhaps Zech. 12:10), Ps. 51:13, and 143:10, among the variously reported activities of the Spirit there are none named which belong to the moral or religious sphere. The same is true of the prophets' self-estimate. We immediately assume that they distinguished themselves by a lofty piety, a love for their people eager to sacrifice, and we gain a deep impression of this in the reading of their writings, particularly their prayers. Their righteousness before God and men is not without value for their prophetic calling. Unclean lips cannot proclaim the words of the Holy One of Israel (Isa. 6), and what the prophets regard as a task from Yahweh is at the same time their own moral conviction. The mighty force of their words, still deeply affecting the reader today, is borne by their consciousness of proclaiming "justice" (Mic. 3:8). Precisely at this point such prophets as Elijah and Isaiah are set apart

13. See the temptation narrative and Acts 16:16; Shepherd of Hermas, Mandate 11; *Didache* 11; Lucianus *Peregrinus Proteus* 11.

from the seers of Israel and other peoples. But they do not trace their own religious and moral life to the Spirit. The Spirit confers on them a higher understanding; he gives them a task and authority to announce it to the people. He also gives the energy to pursue their prophetic calling unshaken, but in other respects he does not confer a conduct pleasing to God. For the prophets too the doing of justice and righteousness is still everyone's affair; it is merely the prerequisite for the prophetic office. Thus, according to the prophets' own assertion, the power in which the רוח is manifest in them can only in a limited sense be called "originality in the sphere of religion."[14] What they possessed from the Spirit was instead originality in religious perception. Wendt's opinion must be judged by this rule:

> Actually, only in the older histories, particularly in the sagalike narratives of Judges, do we find the Spirit of God conceived in this ecstatic form; in the prophetic books, traces of such a view appear only in quite isolated passages; to great extent even the prophetic activities of the Spirit in the narrower sense . . . give way to other moral, religious activities, which are especially (and that must mean *only*) assigned to the messianic king and the community of the awaited end time.[15]

If we compare the small number of prophetic passages cited above which assign religious and moral activities to the Spirit of God with the much greater number of those which refer to activities not belonging in this sphere, then we cannot conceive how a judgment that reverses this relationship could arise.[16]

We can observe the same thing in the extracanonical literature of Judaism, provided we first disregard The Wisdom of Solomon and the Testaments of the Twelve Patriarchs. Naturally, there is very little said

---

14. Wendt, *Begriffe*, p. 33.

15. Ibid., p. 152.

16. The actual situation is as follows (I list only those passages the interpretation of which appears to me to be certain): 4 passages in the prophets, with moral and religious activities of the Spirit (Isa. 11:2; 32:15; 28:6; Ezek. 36:27); 7 passages in which the Spirit of God works in ecstatic fashion (Ezek. 11:24; 3:12; 8:3; 11:1; 43:5; 3:14; 37:1); in 13 passages the genuinely prophetic activities (Isa. 61:1; 63:10–11; 63:14; 48:16; 59:21; 30:1; 42:1; Zech. 7:12; Haggai 2:5; Joel 3:1–2; Hos. 9:7; Mic. 3:8; Ezek. 11:5). The ratio of those passages that contain moral and religious activities of the Spirit to those which derive other activities from the Spirit of Yahweh is thus 4 to 20 or 1 to 5!

of the Holy Spirit here, but it is precisely this that yields a typical proof for the accuracy of our assertion. Particularly in those writings that treat average piety and morality, as does Sirach, the Spirit does not appear as a present possession. Righteous conduct has nothing to do with the Spirit. Where the literature of Judaism refers to activities of the Spirit, the concern is almost always with prophecy, vision, wisdom, and so on (see Sir. 48:24; Sus. 42:64, LXX;[17] Ps. Sol. 8:15;[18] 4 Ezra 14:22;[19] Apoc. Bar. 6;[20] En. 56:5; 68:2; 71:5,11; 91:1;[21] Bk. Jub. 25:31;[22] Asmp. M.[23] 11:34,[24] chap. 17, and elsewhere).

Worthy of special note is the fact that such activities of the Spirit are for the most part events of long ago. Precisely here, at the very outset of our investigation we see that Judaism distinguished itself from ancient Israel and from the Christian community by the fact that it produced no or, stated more cautiously, only very few pneumatic phenomena. In essence, then, we are compelled to construct our analogies to New Testament ideas from the Old Testament.

IS THE VALUE OF AN APPEARANCE A SYMPTOM OF THE SPIRIT'S INFLUENCE?

We have found that in primitive Christianity only a portion of the activities of the Spirit are assigned direct status and worth in Christian conduct. Do all the gifts of the Spirit have at least indirect significance for the Christian life, influencing it by promoting these gifts? Until now, this question has not yet been expressly put or answered. But indeed, all agree that it must obviously be answered in the affirmative. Thus Weiss writes, "Naturally, these gifts of the Spirit are not at all to

17. In the Susanna theodicy there is no reference to the Spirit of God, contra Gloël, *Der heilige Geist,* p. 231, n. 2.
18. Edited by Adolf Hilgenfeld in *Messias Judaeorum* (Leipzig, 1869).
19. "Ezras propheta latine" in ibid.
20. In *Monumenta Sacra et Profana,* tom. 1, fasc. 2 (Milan, 1861).
21. Trans. C.F.A. Dillmann (Leipzig, 1853).
22. Trans. Dillmann in Heinrich Ewald, *Jahrbücher der biblischen Wissenschaft,* 2d and 3d ed. (Göttingen, 1850), p. 51.
23. "Assumptio Mosis," ed. Hilgenfeld in *Messias Judaeorum.*
24. Ed. Gustav Volkmar, *Mose Prophetie und Himmelfahrt* (Leipzig, 1867).

be construed as merely 'miraculous phenomena,' but rather as the equipping of God's servants for the work required of them."[25] This is also the position of Hermann Cremer, Wendt, Otto Pfleiderer, Gloël, et al.[26]

With respect to the majority of the gifts of the Spirit we will immediately concur with the foregoing judgments. Just consider the preaching of Jesus and his disciples, or the miracles confirming their preaching, as inspired by the Spirit. But our concern here is with what is common to all the activities of the Spirit. Our question must read: Is it a symptom of a pneumatic phenomenon that it exercises an especially valuable effect on the eye- or ear-witnesses, an effect recognized by religious persons to be its divine purpose and on account of which the pneumatic source of the phenomenon is inferred?

Here if anywhere it is of greatest importance to distinguish the original event and its evaluation at the time of its occurrence from the narrative and evaluation of the later narrator. It is obvious that each historical writer pragmatizes, that his narrative refers to causes and effects though in most imperfect fashion. Further, it is obvious that each author who views history in a religious sense regards the effect of a phenomenon as the purpose intended by God. The latter, subsequent perception, however necessary for religious people, need not influence us at all in our investigation. We must rather raise this question: Did those who experienced the pneumatic appearances or observed them as eyewitnesses identify them as pneumatic because those appearances struck them as having a special purpose that they served in an especially perfect way and, according to God's decree, should serve? In other words, are the activities of the Spirit miracles in Schleiermacher's terms or in terms of supernaturalism?

Let us imagine what was in Peter's soul from the situation depicted in Acts 10:19. Whether this is legend or at least embellished in sagalike fashion does not concern us, since it is well known that precisely in sagas the religious views of a period emerge with special clarity. Peter has received the vision of the great sheet with all kinds of beasts.

25. Weiss, *Lehrbuch*, p. 60, n. 2; p. 595; p. 129, n. 1.
26. *Realencyclopädie für protestantische Theologie und Kirche* (Leipzig, 1906), 5:12; Wendt, *Begriffe*, p. 51; Pfleiderer, *Urchristentum*, p. 255 ("for special purposes"); Gloël, *Der heilige Geist*, pp. 322–23.

While he is still pondering the meaning of this vision the Spirit says to him: "Behold, three men are looking for you. Rise and go down, and accompany them without hesitation; for I have sent them." The Spirit thus gives Peter information and a command. Peter immediately recognizes that both come from the Spirit, for in verse 21 he immediately obeys the instruction given him. He cannot have recognized the voice as God's from the purpose of the command, for the Spirit's intention is clear to him only in what follows (vv. 22ff.; 30ff.), that is, the first missionary preaching to the Gentiles. And even if he had known the desire of the men who came to him—which, according to the narrator, is evidently not the case (see v. 29)—it is not on account of their content and purpose that he would have judged as "spiritual" the words which an unknown power whispered to him. For our narrative clearly does not infer from the admittedly legitimate preaching to the Gentiles that the initial decision to preach to them derives from God. Rather, justification for the Gentile mission is inferred from a command to preach to the Gentiles which is acknowledged to be divine (see Acts 15:8,14).

Thus, in the matter of the vision narrated in Acts 10:19, we find that although the narrator knows all too well the divine purpose of the wondrous appearance, the person acting in the narrative does not infer the activity of the Spirit as such from any recognizable purpose. So the subject does not perceive a pneumatic appearance when he feels most intensely that it corresponds perfectly to God's intentions and purposes, that is, when at this point he thinks he understands God's rule over the world with total clarity. Rather, although he does not always know to what purpose God has effected this appearance, its divine origin is still clear from other symptoms. The idea of the Spirit does not at all cohere in a religious evaluation of history led by God toward its hallowed goal.

This generalizing on an observation drawn from one example is fully justified where it is a matter of reading symptoms that would apply in every case. But for greater surety let us consider still other activities of the Spirit in light of our question.

A quite similar activity occurs in Acts 16:6. Paul is hindered by the Holy Spirit from proclaiming the word in Asia, even from entering Bithynia. It is clearly the narrator's view that by this action the Spirit intended to lead the apostle to Troas and from there to Europe. According to the narrative, Paul himself knew nothing of this intent. Weiss actually thinks that the guidance of the Spirit had as its aim a dispensing with apostolic activity wherever Jewish-Christian communities already existed.[27] But quite apart from the accuracy of that assertion, loaned from 1 Pet. 1:1, what clearly militates against this view of the Spirit's guiding is that according to Acts 16:7 Paul and his co-travelers did not at first recognize the Spirit's intent but sought to learn his will by experimentation. Paul was thus firmly convinced that the mysterious instructions he received derived from the Spirit of Jesus, for he obeyed without delay. He bowed to the divine command without knowing its purpose. So here too divine authorship is not inferred from the content or purpose of such a mysterious command, however worthy of the divine.

The case is similar with Simeon in Luke 2:27. In the opinion of the narrator, Simeon may have been aware of what the Spirit intended when he led him into the temple. There he was to experience the fulfillment of the promise given him and behold the infant Redeemer of his people. At the same time—as the narrator for his part conceives it—the Spirit selected him to render the Messiah that first homage of the Israel which awaited him. But while Simeon recognized as divine and carried out the summons given him to go into the temple because the Messiah was there, this did not occur because of a content or purpose that was clearly worthy of the divine. That content could be false and the purpose unattainable. Other symptoms made him certain that it was the Spirit speaking to him, quite apart from the content and intent of the commands. On the other hand, if the ἔρχεσθαι ἐν τῷ πνεύματι should be construed, as in Acts 16:6, as an obscure impulse, then it is also clear in this case that when Simeon viewed it as pneumatic and yielded to it, he knew nothing of the intent of the Spirit and thus could not have traced the divine intent of this appearance to its author.

The apocalyptist who asserts he received his revelations ἐν πνεύματι is convinced of their divine origin, and demands that his visions be so understood, not because everyone who consoles and warns the church

---

27. Bernhard Weiss, *Lehrbuch der neutestamentlichen Einleitung* (Berlin, 1886), p. 143.

is a prophet of God. For if his revelations were tested by this measure, much could be shown which neither consoles nor warns but simply predicts the future and would still have been totally useless to the seven churches had its pneumatic origin not been established. For him the divine inspiration of his book stands firm apart from any purpose, since he recognized the Spirit's power from other symptoms. And the esteem given the book is explained only by the fact that the oldest readers believed the author when he wrote that he was ἐν πνεύματι. They themselves had no indication by which to establish the book's inspiration. The lie may also console.

The same is true of the prophecies narrated in Acts 11:27ff., 20:23, and 21:10–11 and which Paul utters in Rom. 11:25ff. and 1 Cor. 15:23ff. (2 Thess. 2:3ff.). It is not because of the divine purpose to support the brethren in Judea that Agabus's prophecy of a great famine coming over the whole earth was perceived as pneumatic. Rather, because there were other reasons for regarding his prophecy as taking place διὰ τοῦ πνεύματος, and that for these reasons the famine was inevitable, money was collected in Christian love for the support of the brethren. Thus in the view of the New Testament age, prophecy was not recognized as such because its divine intent was noted. The judgment that such and such a prophecy stems from the Spirit does not in the least depend upon the ascertainment of its purpose.

It is well known that among the gifts of the Spirit glossolalia occupies a special place. It was glossolalia that at Pentecost first revealed the Spirit's descent upon the believers. In the later conversations in Acts 10:44ff. and 19:6, it plays an equally prominent role. In Acts 15:8 the occurrence of glossolalic speech at Cornelius's conversion is cited as proof that in giving the Spirit God makes no distinction between Gentile and Jewish Christian. It is clear from 1 Corinthians that this community also ranked glossolalia extraordinarily high. How would the estimate of just such a gift have been possible if what was especially valuable for the edification of the church was universally regarded as an activity of the Spirit? This much surely follows from Paul's description, that of all the Spirit's gifts the one least valuable for the life of the church was glossolalia.

All these examples support our thesis that the consciousness of a special divine purpose did not belong to the symptoms of an activity of the Spirit, that for this reason what is of worth to the community must not on that account be an activity of the Spirit.

This contention has support especially from what is not said in the narrative of the Spirit's activities. If it were true, as is almost always tacitly assumed, that to each activity of the Spirit there belongs a divine purpose by which it is known as such, then we could not understand why the narrators are so often silent about this purpose, or, when a particularly religious perception gives way to the purely historical, why they are silent about the effect the manifestations of the Spirit had on eyewitnesses.

By what means do the Jewish-Christian eyewitnesses to the event narrated in Acts 10:44 know that it is precisely the Holy Spirit who is suddenly and unexpectedly poured out on the Gentiles converted by Peter's sermon? "For they heard them speaking in tongues and extolling God" (v. 46). It is obviously not because of the great effect speaking in tongues has on anyone but because of the undeniable fact of that speaking as such that they conclude the Gentiles have received the Spirit. The same is true in Acts 19:6. Nor is the situation any different in Acts 15:8. Speaking in tongues as such is already sufficient proof of the Spirit's activity within the sphere of the Gentile mission and is totally apart from the effect of the miraculous occurrence. This acknowledged activity of the Spirit is a legitimation as valid as are the signs and wonders reported in Acts 15:12.

Jesus' response to the messengers from John the Baptist in Matt. 11:2ff. is in full accord with these observations. Jesus replies to the question whether he is the Messiah not by orienting the Baptist to the salutary effects of his deeds on the Jewish people but by describing his works to him. By these John may know well enough that in Jesus the Spirit promised by the prophets is at work. These works are an ἀπόδειξις πνεύματος καὶ δυνάμεως. Again, only the activities of the Spirit themselves, not their further result, provide the symptom.

Certain phenomena are *eo ipso* viewed as spiritual, though their purpose is often not seen at all, or at least is not spoken of. The comparison of the Spirit with the wind in John 3:8 best agrees with this. Just as the coming and going of the wind is an enigma, so it is with the Spirit. Like the wind, the Spirit mocks all human calculation.

"You do not know whence it comes or whither it goes." One can as little understand the Spirit's purpose as the way of the wind in the air. But just as one hears the voice of the wind and thereby recognizes its presence, so one can perceive the Spirit from his effects.

Let us compare the Old Testament narratives of the Spirit's activities. For the Old Testament too evaluations are given which are almost in direct proportion to those cited above for the New Testament.[28] It is easy to understand that the narrators very often supposed they could recognize the divine purposes of the Spirit's activities in the course of their story. Thus the narrator of Judg. 9:23ff. knew why Yahweh caused discord between Abimelech and the men of Shechem through an evil spirit. It occurred in order to atone for the bloodguilt that both parties equally shared. There is similar material in Exod. 31:3-4 and 35:31-32, and in Num. 11:17 the Spirit can actually be called the bestowal of the office of the seventy. In Isa. 61:1ff. and 42:1ff. the Servant of Yahweh is given the Spirit that he משפט לגוים יוציא, and in Isa. 28:6 the former rulers are promised the Spirit to help further Israel's deliverance from within and without. But these passages, of course, only make clear that in his activities, God's Spirit may often have an explicit or easily recognizable purpose, not that he must.

But what significance is there for God's purposes in Israel when in Judg. 14:6 the Spirit comes upon Samson in the vineyards of Timnah so that he tears a lion asunder as one tears a kid? Here it is still clear that the descent of Yahweh's Spirit is recognized by quite different symptoms than by any purpose. When, further, in Judg. 15:14 the Spirit of Yahweh suddenly falls on the bound and captive Samson so that he tears his ropes asunder and kills one thousand Philistines, here too it is simply the superhuman deed as such which is taken to be an activity of the Spirit, without the narrator's least thought of assigning to Samson's surprising victory any significance for the history of Israel or the tribe of Dan.

---

28. Wendt, *Begriffe,* p. 140: "for special purposes"; Pfleiderer, *Urchristentum,* p. 255: "for specific purposes"; Paul Kleinert, *Zur alttestamentlichen Lehre vom Geist Gottes, Jahrbuch für deutsche Theologie: 1867,* p. 31: "for the service of the kingdom of God"; Schultz, *Alttestamentliche Theologie,* pp. 546-47: "as the moral conditions or the purposes of the kingdom of God require."

There is just as little reference to any purposeful activity of the Spirit in 1 Sam. 10:6ff. and 19:20ff. This is quite clear when we recall that the התנבא, so vividly described in 1 Sam. 19:20ff., was originally an ecstatic raving. First Kings 18:7ff. is also of special interest here. Obadiah, an official of King Ahab, is ordered by Elijah to tell his master that the prophet is present. Obadiah protests, "Wherein have I sinned, that you would give your servant into the hand of Ahab, to kill me? . . . As soon as I have gone from you, the Spirit of the Lord will carry you whither I know not; and so, when I come and tell Ahab and he cannot find you, he will kill me." Hence Obadiah thinks it is possible, indeed even likely, that Elijah, seized by the Spirit and contrary to the meeting just arranged, will leave the place at which he is presently stopping. In his view Elijah's conduct is quite unpredictable since he is not his own master but under a higher authority whose purposes are unknown. Obadiah, then, does not share the view that the function of the Spirit might be a conscious, purposeful activity on Yahweh's behalf. He conceives the Spirit's activities as totally unpredictable and often apparently without purpose. Second Kings 2:16ff. gives evidence that this view is not unique. The sons of the prophets of Jericho are not really convinced that Yahweh has taken Elijah to himself but think the Spirit of Yahweh may have seized him and thrown him on one of the mountains or in one of the valleys. Here too such miraculous changes of place are expected of the Spirit, and precisely because of their unforeseeable character they are held to be pneumatic. Incidentally, neither passage presents a view that is unique. This notion of the Spirit must have been common in the time of the narrators. It is clear from Dan. 5:11,14 that even in the later Jewish period a special purpose was not reckoned among the symptoms of the Spirit's activity. Naturally, the recognition that Daniel has the רוח אלהין קדישין is placed in the mouth of heathen. But as soon as we substitute the singular for the plural "gods" we have every right to assume a genuinely Jewish idea here. By what means do king and queen perceive that "the spirit of the holy gods" is in Daniel? By the fact that he possesses a special wisdom, manifest, for example, in the interpretation of dreams and the solving of riddles. It is exactly the same view of the Spirit as that which appears in Gen. 41:38, in which Pharaoh says of Joseph, who has just interpreted his dream, "Can we find such a man as this, in whom רוח אלהים בו?'' The ability to interpret dreams as such demonstrates the presence of the Spirit. And as to the purposes of the spiritual gifts—*altum silentium.*

One of the most telling proofs that in the Old Testament the ascertainment of an activity of the Spirit cannot rest on its known divine purpose is the fact that in the older literature of Israel not only good but also harm, even evil, is thought to be caused by the "Spirit of God" or by an "evil spirit from the Lord" (רוח יהוה רעה appears only once in 1 Sam. 19:9).[29] We moderns are quite eager to render intelligible this idea that at first seems alien by thinking that harmful activities from the Spirit of God are attributed to him only because they also are supposed to serve Yahweh's saving intent with his people. But on closer examination this expedient is impossible. For example, it is obvious from 1 Sam. 16:14ff. that Saul's servants, who regard their king's melancholy (sometimes raised to madness) as the activity of an evil spirit from God (v. 15), are not at all aware that Saul's depression may be Yahweh's means of withdrawing the crown from him and his dynasty for Israel's good. The entire subsequent narrative, dealing with the battles of the Saulites against David, indicates that Saul's warriors at that time did not yet entertain such a passive view of things. Thus, without their being aware of any purpose for it, the depression is derived from an evil spirit of God. The same applies to 1 Sam. 18:10 and 19:9. Now, as de Visser[30] remarks, this ancient notion that harmful, even sinful, activities may proceed from the divine Spirit soon became offensive, since it had to conflict with the conviction of enlightened thought touching Yahweh's holiness— evidenced by the fact that the evil spirit is not generally called רוח יהוה רעה. Indeed, 1 Kings 22:19ff. specifically contrasts him with the רוח יהוה. So in a later period we no longer find such expressions. When in Ps. Sol. 8:15 the surprising reception that the Jewish leaders give Pompey in Palestine is traced to a πνεῦμα πλανήσεως, then this πνεῦμα cannot at all be identified with the πνεῦμα ἅγιον. In the New Testament there is scarcely any echo of the ancient idea of God's

29. See Johannes T. de Visser, *De daemonologie van het Oude Testament* (Utrecht, 1880), pp. 5ff., 14ff.
30. Ibid., pp. 14ff., 30ff.

29

Spirit as working also what is harmful, since the πνεῦμα κατανύξεως in Rom. 11:8 appears only in quotation, and the ἐνέργεια πλάνης of 2 Thess. 2:11 must be taken in the same sense as Ps. Sol. 8:15. Though Paul, with his powerful religious energy, does not think it absurd to derive even evil from God (Rom. 1:24; 5:20; 11:25), he still does not connect this idea with the notion of the divine Spirit, however nearly it might have lain in 2 Thess. 2:11. Rather, in later Jewish literature and in the New Testament such appearances are traced to Satan and his demons. For this reason we may not simply transfer to the New Testament the original view just mentioned, but it does show us most clearly that ancient Israel did not think to infer the source of a phenomenon in the Spirit of Yahweh from its worthwhile effect, and that though only the basic features of the Old Testament idea are retained in the New, the judgment of the New Testament age that a phenomenon is brought about by the Spirit may not be taken as a judgment as to value.

SYMPTOMS OF THE SPIRIT'S INFLUENCE

Marks of Individual Activities of the Spirit

If we intend to understand the view of the Spirit cherished by the apostolic age, then we must begin from the Spirit's most striking and characteristic activity, that of glossolalia. It has already been noted that glossolalia played an especially prominent role in the Corinthian community. It is often stated that preference at Corinth for this very gift harks back to the influence of a pagan religious view. Thus Weizsäcker sees in the Corinthian practice of glossolalia "an exercise of wild enthusiasm that assumes a person is closer to God when he is out of his mind" and reckons it to manifestations "of the ancient and not yet mastered pagan spirit."[31] Heinrici holds a similar view.[32] These statements are irrefutable. As Christians, the glossolalics in Corinth transferred to the πνεῦμα their earlier view of the divine activity. Only when we assume this can we see why the πνεῦμα could be so vital to the Corinthians and could produce such a welter of

31. Weizsäcker, *Zeitalter,* p. 298.
32. Heinrici, *Sendschreiben,* p. 350.

phenomena. But we may not draw the conclusion that such an estimate of glossolalia is specifically ethnic. The same estimate is also found in the sources of Acts, though the author, as is certain from Acts 2, no longer recognized the phenomenon. But we are clearly in the right when we use just this gift to establish the symptoms of the Spirit's activity, since it must have been widely regarded as the spiritual gift par excellence. The usage yields proof of this. In 1 Cor. 14:37 πνευματικός in contrast to προφήτης—an especially noteworthy instance—clearly denotes glossolalia. Likewise, in 1 Thess. 5:19 πνεῦμα is set next to προφητεία as the capacity for speaking in tongues. Πνεῦμα is used in the same sense in 2 Thess. 2:2. We can see how firmly rooted this usage must have been even in Paul's day, since even he takes it up, though when he follows his own usage he gives the term πνευματικός in 1 Cor. 2:15 and 3:1 an entirely different sense. Clearly the reason for this striking usage must have been that the symptoms of the presence of the divine Spirit were most clearly and conspicuously present in glossolalia. This can be compared with the התנבא of the Old Testament—in its original sense closely related to glossolalia—and described in Num. 11:25 and 1 Sam. 10:6, 10, 18:10, and 19:20ff. as ecstatic raving. Such behavior, as is clear from Num. 11:25, is viewed as that manifestation of the Spirit in which the descent of the divine is most easily and directly perceived. So it is not enough to say that glossolalia was the most conspicuous gift of the Spirit—it was at the same time the most characteristic.

Modern scholars have not yet reached agreement on the original meaning of the term *glossolalia*. But these days there is scarcely any difference of opinion as to the nature of the phenomenon itself. The interpretation of a speaking in foreign languages (according to Acts 2) has now been set aside, and Paul's characterization of the phenomenon is still clear enough that we can hardly be in doubt as to its nature. Thus contemporary debate over the meaning of the term need not concern us here.

In glossolalia the individual is overwhelmed by a powerful force that has taken total possession of him. In such situations he is passive. He himself is no longer agent; instead, something alien has come over him and added to his independent, personal life. What Chrysostom writes of μάντις also gives a vivid description of ancient glossolalia:

τοῦτο γὰϱ μάντεως ἴδιον, τὸ ἐξεστηκέναι, τὸ ἀνάγκην ὑπομένειν, τὸ ὠθεῖσθαι, τὸ ἕλκεσθαι, τὸ σύϱεσθαι ὥσπεϱ μαινόμενον.[33] Thus the person cannot give to the emotions that move him so mightily a clear expression which is intelligible to all, and even when he has come to himself again he is not immediately able to describe his experiences to others. The irreverent spectator pronounced the verdict that the glossolalics are mad (1 Cor. 14:23) or full of new wine (Acts 2:13). The condition is thus compared to drunkenness or insanity. This similarity obviously consists in the fact that the glossolalic speaks in such a way that the usual speech of a rational person cannot be recognized. But when in such instances the Christian sees the working of the divine Spirit, then he too is convinced that something is taking place which could not be explained by the normal psychic condition of an ordinary person. And while he regards irreverent interpretations of glossolalia as blasphemies, he too perceives in this phenomenon something abnormal, a mystery, which someone could not produce by himself. In glossolalia one speaks "mysteries" that others do not understand (1 Cor. 14:2), which one himself could not utter if the Spirit did not reveal them.

According to this rule, the symptoms needed to identify an activity of the Spirit are to be defined. It is the mysterious and the overwhelming in human life which is derived from the Spirit of God. Hence the apostolic age recognizes certain phenomena that manifest a power which "fills" a person, that is, which so completely possesses a person that he often becomes its all but unwilling instrument. They are occurrences that seem to defy every explanation by natural powers inherent in man; and precisely because they cannot be derived from the world or from human nature, they are regarded as being of divine origin, as activities of the Spirit.[34]

To review, an activity of the Spirit is ascertained not within the scheme of means and ends but rather within the scheme of cause and effect. Belief in the Spirit is not for the purpose of grasping God's

33. Chrysostom, *Hom. XXIX ad I Cor. 12:2,* in Friedrich Bleek, *Einleitung ins Alte Testament,* 4th ed. (Berlin, 1878), p. 315.

34. See Justini M. *Cohort. ad Graecos* 8, in which the reference οὔτε γὰϱ φύσει οὔτε ἀνθϱωπίνη ἐννοίᾳ οὕτω μεγάλα καὶ θεῖα γινώσκειν ἀνθϱώποις δυνατόν, ἀλλὰ τῇ ἄνωθεν ἐπὶ τοὺς ἁγίους ἄνδϱας τηνικαῦτα κατελθούσῃ (according to Albrecht Ritschl, *Die Altkatholische Kirche,* 2d ed. [Bonn, 1857], p. 472) is first of all to prophets.

plan for the world but for the purpose of explaining the presence of certain, above all inexplicable, phenomena by means of the transcendent.

The ecstasy of the apocalyptist referred to in Rev. 1:10 and 4:2 and the revelations referred to in Gal. 2:2, 2 Cor. 12:1, Acts 13:2, 9:3ff., and elsewhere are most closely related to glossolalia. These also are received ἐν πνεύματι. At issue here are spiritual occurrences in which the person cannot witness to the spontaneous expressions of an inner life known to him. He does not cause the words he thinks he hears (2 Cor. 12:4,9), the thoughts that rush in on him in such instances (Gal. 2:2), the visions he sees (Acts 7:55; 2 Cor. 12:1), or the volitions irresistibly forcing themselves on him (Acts 13:2). He is fully aware that they are given to him from without, by something alien to him. He himself was not the actor but rather the recipient, passive, seized and "caught up"[35] by something mighty. An excess of visions claims a person to the extent that the reflective activity of his intellect, though not at complete rest as in glossolalia, is nonetheless diminished and cannot pursue the transcendent experiences with any certainty (2 Cor. 12:2). For this reason the person who experiences such phenomena is convinced that a higher power stronger than himself overtook him, and he concludes, "The Spirit of God has given this to me."

Acts 16:6ff., 20:22, and Luke 2:27, 4:1,14 are also to be construed in this fashion. (Is the πνεῦμα of Acts 8:29 the ὁ ἄγγελος κυρίου of v. 26?) At issue here are impulses that overwhelm with an unlimited force (Acts 16:6) so that the person feels "bound" by the power resting on him (Acts 20:22). He cannot but carry out whatever this mysterious power inspires in him, though he may be aware of the danger into which he is falling. On the other hand, he distinguishes himself most clearly from the power that controls him (Acts 16:7, ἐπείραζον). What else can this power be, inexplicable in terms of his own psychic existence and yet total master of him, if not the power that is not from men but from the divine Spirit?

Thus the inexplicable and the overwhelming are symptoms of the

---

35. See 2 Cor. 12:2; Apoc. Bar. 6: *sustulit me et extulit;* En. 39:3; 52:1; 71:5; and in particular the vivid description in En. 14:8. In sagalike and embellished fashion, Acts 8:39 describes rapture ἐν πνεύματι, in ecstasy, as a physical transfer by the Spirit of the Lord.

Spirit's appearing, and in the apostolic era whenever a person thinks he is witness to a force that cannot be explained by conditions prevailing in the world he infers the presence of the Spirit. A miracle is something that the Spirit works. The counterpart to this idea would be ἰδίᾳ δυνάμει (Acts 3:12) or ἐξ ἀνθρώπων (Matt. 21:25). To the ἀφ᾽ ἑαυτοῦ λέγειν in John 11:51 (see Ezek. 13:3) is contrasted the προφητεύειν. The relationship between divine and human activity is that of mutually exclusive opposition. The activity of the Spirit is thus not an intensifying of what is native to all. It is rather the absolutely supernatural and hence divine. If over against the Spirit the person can only be regarded as a passive recipient (παθεῖν, Gal. 3:4), somehow, by his own action, he may still prepare himself to receive the Spirit. Thus in Acts 13:2 a manifestation of the Spirit is given on the occasion of prayer and fasting (see Luke 2:37; 1 Tim. 5:5).[36] When Paul readily admits to his Corinthians that they "are zealous for spirits"[37] but exhorts them earnestly to desire the higher gifts (1 Cor. 12:31), to strive to excel in building up the church (1 Cor. 14:12)—to desire prophecy (1 Cor. 14:39) and glossolalia (14:13; see also 2 Tim. 1:6, ἀναζωπυρεῖν τὸ χάρισμα)—then he still assumes that in receiving the spiritual gifts the person is not merely passive but in some fashion autonomous, though only in the appropriation of the gifts.[38] There is nothing to indicate that the apostolic period experienced any contradiction in these two lines of thought, that is, that the Spirit of God is a free gift and by his own free will gives to each his charisma (1 Cor. 12:11) and that one can and should still earnestly "desire" the gifts of grace. Both statements can be made side by side. Rational reflection as

36. See Dan. 10:2ff.; 4 Ezra 5:13,20; 6:31,35; 9:24ff.; Apoc. Bar. 12:20; 43(47); Jth. 11:17,19; Bk. Jub. 12; Shepherd of Hermas, Vision II, 2:1; III, 1:2, etc.; and the Oracle of Prisca, see Harnack, *Lehrbuch,* p. 357, n. 5; Gottlieb Nathanael Bonwetsch, *Geschichte des Montanismus* (Erlangen, 1881), p. 198. See also the first of the sources underlying chaps. 16–28 of the *Didascalia apostolorum,* ed. Adolf von Harnack in *Texte und Untersuchungen,* vol. 2, no. 5, p. 22, and the Muratorian Fragment *sub ev. Joh.;* Tertullian, *De ieiunio* 12; and *Passio Perpetua* 4. 7, cited by Harnack on the passage. Hermann Lüdemann, *Anthropologie des Apostels Paulus* (Kiel, 1872), p. 35, n. 4, regards the notion of a preparation for revelation as Hellenistic!

37. According to Heinrici, *Sendschreiben,* p. 438.

38. A similar view is expressed in Rom. 12:3,6: The measure of the gift of each Christian is conditional upon the measure of faith given him by God (v. 3). This rule is reiterated in v. 6 of prophecy, "the" most significant gift, since it assumes an especially powerful faith.

to how the two could rhyme was not arrived at because a person did not so much reflect upon as live in the Spirit. We should further note that the term ζηλοῦν, used by Paul of the autonomy of the Spirit-bearer, is uncommonly weighty and denotes a striving by the mustering up of all one's energy of will—for which reason we cannot agree with Heinrici, who thinks the term is chosen with "caution."[39] At the same time, this word may have reached the apostle through a letter from the church (1 Cor. 14:12, ἐπεὶ ζηλωταί ἐστε πνευμάτων). Whether or not the gifts of the Spirit were totally or only in part supernatural has also been a matter of debate. According to the view of the apostolic age, everything held to be a gift of the Spirit is of supernatural origin. But how we moderns would judge such phenomena through our perception of the world does not belong to the sphere of a purely historical investigation.

Accordingly, it is clear what the apostolic age had in mind by the term *Spirit*. It is the supernatural power of God which works miracles in and through the person. Everything we have learned of the activities of the Spirit witnesses to the appropriateness of this definition.

If wisdom is derived from the Spirit then it is a wisdom only few Christians possess (Acts 6:3; 1 Cor. 12:8). This wisdom enables the one to whom it is given to overcome the objections of his enemies (Acts 6:10; 2 Cor. 10:4ff.). Such an extraordinary, irresistible wisdom that shows its superiority over ordinary worldly wisdom in such a way cannot come from this world. It can only be an activity of the Spirit. Or this wisdom is a matter of understanding the highest truths, of a profound penetration of the mysteries of God (1 Cor. 2:7-10), a capacity that cannot be explained from out of oneself but must be assigned to something higher. This is no longer a wisdom τοῦ αἰῶνος τούτου—God has revealed it through the Spirit (1 Cor. 2:6-10). Thus, even teachers who declaim with such wisdom are viewed as inspired (1 Cor. 12:28; Rom. 12:7; Eph. 4:11).[40]

Paul distinguishes σοφία and γνῶσις in 1 Cor. 12:8. But this dif-

---

39. Heinrici, *Sendschreiben,* p. 410, n. 3.

40. The deriving of wisdom from the Spirit indicates that even for the early Christian view the concepts "pneumatic" and "ecstatic" are not identical. In one instance the Spirit is at work without being intelligible to consciousness. In the other the Spirit totally penetrates it (according to Weizsäcker, *Zeitalter,* p. 117). Therefore, Harnack's description of the πνεῦμα *(Lehrbuch,* 1:47, n. 1) is not quite correct.

ference is of no concern to us since it is our task not to indicate what the characteristic of each individual gift is but to describe what is universally pneumatic.

The prophet is filled with the Spirit. The Spirit whispers secret revelations in the prophet's ear and informs him of things no human intelligence could know. So the Spirit makes known to Agabus that a famine will come over all the world (Acts 11:28) or that Paul will be chained at Jerusalem and delivered into the hands of the Gentiles (Acts 21:10ff.). Paul himself can preach the mystery of the hardening and eventual conversion of his people (Rom. 11:25–26) or with the eye of a seer can survey the imminent end of this aeon (1 Cor. 15:51ff.,23ff.). The Corinthian prophets have at their disposal a superhuman knowledge of the secrets of the human heart (1 Cor. 14:24ff.; see John 4:18ff.). These revelations, unattainable by any human intelligence, must be imparted by something that is transcendent. They are announced in enraptured sentences that erupt from the breast with such elemental force that the person can hardly keep silent (1 Cor. 14:23–24), and they evoke in the listener an overwhelmingly shattering impression (1 Cor. 14:24–25). This makes clear that prophecy assumes an especially high intensity of faith (Rom. 12:6).[41]

In addition, an especially robust faith is traced to the Spirit, a faith that does not give way in persecutions but shows its superior power particularly when the Christian must answer before the tribunal. Then the words rush into him and he need not carefully consider beforehand what he shall say. In the decisive moment he feels the motion of that divine power which allows him to speak with great inspiration and confidence of success (Mark 13:11; Matt. 10:19,20; Luke 12:11–12; Acts 4:13,31). Or it is a faith that proves its power in special, miraculous signs (Matt. 17:9–10; 1 Cor. 13:2; 12:9; 2 Cor. 4:13).

There are external miracles as well—healings, even raisings from the dead—for which the Spirit gives power to human beings (1 Cor. 12:9–10). Indeed, these are evidence of a dominion over nature not given to ordinary mortals. And there are exorcisms, for by what might

41. See above, n. 38.

could one otherwise conquer his celestial foes if not in the power of the Holy Spirit?

There is also the power to discern the guidance of the Holy Spirit from the activities of other spirits. Knowing, for example, whether or not the seemingly Spirit-filled prophets and glossolalics are actually filled with an evil spirit is viewed as a special gift of grace; it would be too difficult for human understanding. In the same fashion, the ability to interpret the words of glossolalics is valued as a pneumatic gift. The words gushing forth under the Spirit's power are often so obscure, so sporadic, that one can only evaluate and understand the "mysteries" uttered in the Spirit when the Spirit himself gives authentic explanation (1 Cor. 12:10). When the New Testament age contends that Holy Scripture is inspired by God it means that the Old Testament is conceived not as a human writing but as the words of God himself.[42] "Through the mouth of David" and other holy men the Spirit prophesied concerning Jesus and the end time (Acts 1:16). The authors are a more or less impartial tool—the one truly at work was the Spirit. So we may assume that knowledge of the mysteries set down in the Scriptures was held to be a gift of the Spirit. Exegesis of the Old Testament was every bit as pneumatic as the interpretation of glossolalia.

According to Paul, the most significant gift of the Spirit is the apostolate (1 Cor. 12:28). This assumes a fullness of the Spirit and includes most of the other gifts. Legitimation by signs and wonders was required of an apostle (2 Cor. 12:12; 1 Thess. 1:5; Rom. 15:18–19; 1 Cor. 2:4), and perhaps also revelations and visions (2 Cor. 12:1).[43] The Pauline letters often give a clear impression of how one must conceive the presence of an apostle, a presence so swollen with spiritual force in word and deed that we can understand why the Gentiles worshiped the apostles as gods come down in the likeness of men (Acts 14:11ff.).

It is not as easy to see why διαχονίαι, ἀντιλήμψεις, and κυβερνήσεις were also regarded as spiritual gifts. The ἀντιλήμψεις, μεταδιδόναι,

---

42. Certainly, the autonomy of the Old Testament authors is differentiated from the perceptions given them by the Spirit (1 Pet. 1:11).

43. See Weizsäcker, *Zeitalter,* p. 609.

and ἐλεεῖν in 1 Cor. 12:28 and Rom. 12:8 must not have been re-garded as ordinary day-to-day, charitable acts that any Christian in any time can and should practice but rather as particularly sacrificial, spontaneous, and magnificent deeds that—as described among the other charismata in 1 Cor. 13:3—did not at all occur outside the Christian community. Or one can locate the pneumatic character of such charitable deeds in the "superior power or wisdom of the ministrants."[44] We may perhaps view the collection that Paul raised in Macedonia for the Jerusalem church as a historical example of such ἀντίλημψις (2 Cor. 8). This yielded so much beyond the abilities of the poor congregations that Paul gives thanks for this gift of God out of a full heart. And the διακονία and κυβερνήσεις—concepts related to the ἀντιλήμψεις—must somehow be construed as justifying the predicate "pneumatic" and thus witness to the divine power in humankind (see 1 Pet. 4–11, εἴ τις διακονεῖ, ὡς ἐξ ἰσχύος, ἧς χορηγεῖ ὁ θεός). At this point where our sources are silent, we can say nothing more precise. In-cidentally, we may not forget that in a fanatically turbulent time the finger of God was readily perceived even in the small and smallest events.

The Impression of the Spirit's Activities

This primitive Christian view of the Spirit was also held in the post-apostolic period, and it persisted in many circles far into the sec-ond century. Local differences may have arisen. Ignatius (*Phila.* 7) most vividly describes a scene he witnessed in Philadelphia. Some members of the congregation oppose Ignatius and attempt to deceive him. Ignatius writes:

> The Spirit is not deceived, for it is from God. For it "knoweth whence it comes and whither it goes" and tests secret things. I cried out while I was with you, I spoke with a great voice, with God's own voice—"Give heed to the bishop, and to the presbytery and deacons." But some suspected me of saying this because I had previous knowledge of the division of some persons; but he in whom I am bound is my witness ὅτι ἀπὸ σαρκὸς ἀν-θρωπίνης οὐκ οἶδα, but the Spirit was preaching.[45]

44. See Heinrici, *Sendschreiben,* p. 409.
45. *The Apostolic Fathers,* trans. Kirsopp Lake, vol. 1, Loeb Classical Library (London: William Heinemann, 1970), pp. 245–47.

Then a few Philadelphians do not allow themselves to be intimidated by Ignatius's warning—suddenly bursting forth "with a great voice, with God's own voice"—and say there is no skill in speaking such words when one is informed beforehand of their schism. But Ignatius asserts that he knew nothing of it beforehand and thus sets down as pneumatic the words suddenly struggling free within him, which so beautifully suited the situation. It is that old view of the πνεῦμα—a supernatural power that suddenly overtakes a person and inspires him with words he could not utter ἀπὸ σαρκὸς ἀνθρωπίνης.

The same view can be clearly seen in the *Didache*. Here too ἐν πνεύματι means to be in ecstasy, just as in Rev. 1:10 and 4:2. And ecstasy is the characteristic form of prophecy. Though this view may also deviate from the New Testament idea of prophecy, most probably from that which Paul assumes in 1 Cor. 14, in any case it witnesses to the survival of the ancient view respecting the symptoms of an activity of the Spirit.

What our sources state of the impression made by the activities of the Spirit on eyewitnesses gives good support to our view of the spiritual gifts. If our conception of the πνεῦμα is correct, namely, that it effects the enigmatic and mighty, then the impression awakened must have been fear mixed with astonishment and hence horror. Here then we can test whether the Spirit was really conceived in the terms we stated above. Of particular concern to us is what is said of the people's reception of Jesus' miracles. It is reported that "they were afraid" (φοβεῖσθαι, φόβος: Matt. 9:8; Mark 5:15; Luke 5:26; 7:16; 8:35), "they were amazed" (ἐξίστασθαι, ἔκστασις: Matt. 12:23; Mark 2:12; 5:42; 6:51; Luke 5:26), "they were astonished" (θάμβος, θαμβεῖσθαι: Mark 1:27; Luke 5:9), "they marveled" (θαυμάζειν: Matt. 8:27; 9:33; 15:31), and "they were shocked" (ἐκπλήττεσθαι: Matt. 13:54; 7:28; Luke 4:32; 9:43), and so on. This is the impression of the deeds of the Spirit. The people see in them something fearful and powerful—both concepts are synonymous for ancient piety (see Shepherd of Hermas, Mandate 7.2: ἐν ᾧ δὲ δύναμις οὐκ ἔστιν, οὐδὲ φόβος, ἐν ᾧ δὲ δύναμις ἡ ἔνδοξος, καὶ φόβος ἐν αὐτῷ)—and something mysterious, inexplicable, and divine. The impression these words give is one that the appearance of the divine on earth generally awakens in ancient man, an impression which, as Isa. 6 and 1 Kings 17:18 clearly indicate, may be linked to the sense of guilt but not simply confused with it.[46]

This graphic view of the Spirit dominates our sources throughout. Wherever the Spirit is spoken of we may assume that the impression described yields the basis for the judgment: the πνεῦμα is ἐπ᾽ αὐτόν. This makes clear that the symptoms of the Spirit's activity are not objectively ascertainable but have only subjective validity, that for this reason varying judgments may be passed on the same event according to the temper of the one who passes judgment. Naturally, this does not mean that those who pass judgment are always conscious of doing so, but at least that they could have no total, inner certainty regarding the reality of the phenomena.

It may be that Acts 15:28 does not give a judgment based on the impression of an appearance. Of course, if the apostolic decree reported there were genuine, it would have to be assumed that the apostles, by handing down the decree, believed they felt a power from above and were thus able to speak on behalf of the Spirit—an idea in itself thoroughly conceivable and unique to primitive Christianity. But if the wording of the decree is a later construction—which we for our part do not doubt—then the Spirit is assigned the apostles at this juncture because, together with their decree, they are credited with a special divine authority. In the latter instance, the later author's judgment that "they had the Spirit in this decision" is a genuine judgment as to value. The case may be similar in Acts 20:28 and 1:2, in which we would note the influence of a later period, an influence amply indicated elsewhere in Acts.

The Spirit and Christ

This Spirit of God—and this is the common conviction of the New Testament age—has made its habitation in the community of Jesus. Activities of the Spirit occur only through Christ to Christians. It is the exalted Lord through whose mediation the Christians receive the Spirit from God. He, already anointed on earth with the Holy Spirit and with power (Acts 10:38) and raised to the right hand of God, has

46. For the impress of the divine in Judaism, see 4 Ezra 5:14; 10:27,30,34ff.; Apoc. Bar. 53; En. 93:11; 106:4; 14:13–14, 24–25; 60:3–4; 65:4; Testament of Levi 3; Bk. Jub. 18.

received the promise of the Holy Spirit from the Father and poured him out upon his disciples (Acts 2:33; Titus 3:6). This surely ancient apostolic concept, also adopted by Paul as we shall see later, is easy to comprehend. Since the exalted One is at once the heavenly protector and regent of his community, that divine power which one rejoices to possess can stem only from him. John 20:22 expresses this thought: The risen (and ascended, 20:17) Lord breathes the Holy Spirit into his disciples. In Rev. 1:1 the apocalyptist names Jesus among the mediators of his revelation, and in Acts 14:3 it is the Lord who allows signs and wonders to occur by the hand of his disciples.

The Spirit a Community Spirit?

If only through Christ, then only to Christians. We may thus call the Spirit the Spirit of the Christian community, a designation, however, which is not from the New Testament and which can very easily be misunderstood. For as we have seen, the concept of the Spirit originally has nothing to do with that of the community. The idea of the community is quite alien to primitive Christianity, if by an appearance one perceives its "spiritual" origin. On the other hand, according to the New Testament the Spirit may not at all be conceived as a product of the community—a notion that easily intrudes itself into the definition given above. The Spirit of God given the community and manifested in signs and wonders is not to be identified with the community spirit of the earliest Christians. A community spirit is both the presupposition and product of a fellowship. But the Holy Spirit of God is neither begotten nor transmitted by human beings, for the One who gives the novice the Spirit is not the missionary who makes converts but is God himself. "The Holy Spirit is God's free gift." In Acts, of course, the view predominates that the Holy Spirit is normally given by the laying on of the apostles' hands (Acts 8:18). But this opinion is hardly an early Christian one. And here as well the laying on of hands is not the cause but the more or less necessary means for the giving of the Spirit. This is true since the ceremony appears to have been accompanied with prayer (Acts 8:15) in which one called on God for the gift of the Spirit. Incidentally, there are reports of outpourings which totally ignore this means (Acts 10:44). Only one thing is agreed to in each instance—that the Spirit descends only upon believers who then are converted through the instrumentality of the community. If, then, according to the primitive Christian view the Spirit is given only through some mediation in the community, every outpouring of the Spirit is nonetheless a new and independent act of God.

Types of Bestowal of the Spirit

In the New Testament age all Christians are generally regarded as filled with the Spirit. This is the characteristic difference between the New Testament and ancient Israel as well as Judaism, which recognize possession of the Spirit only on the part of individuals, and hope for a general outpouring. But the idea that the Spirit is actually given to all members of the Christian community cannot have been the firm, unshakable component of Christian conviction and daily experience, as it was for Paul. Otherwise, use of the term πνευματικός for glossolalia, which inclined one to assign the Spirit only to certain Christians, would be absolutely inexplicable. But even where we encounter the conviction that all Christians have the Spirit, the idea of varying degrees in the apportionment of the Spirit is not ruled out. On the contrary, this idea inheres in the nature of things. The Spirit is given to individuals in varying strengths. Thus, to one person more of the divine gift will be given, to another, less. Hence in 2 Kings 2:9 Elisha prays for two-thirds of the Spirit of Elijah, and in Num. 11:25 God takes the spirit that was on Moses and gives it to the elders of Israel. In the New Testament, Heb. 2:4 speaks of "distributions" of the Holy Spirit. In the same way Acts 2:17 (the quotation is from Joel 3:1, LXX: ἐκχεῶ ἀπὸ τοῦ πνεύματος) and 1 John 4:13 (ἐκ τοῦ πνεύματος αὐτοῦ δέδωκεν ἡμῖν) indicate that the Spirit may be viewed as a substance, a portion of which God has given to Christians. The principle laid down in John 3:34 (οὐ γὰρ ἐκ μέτρου δίδωσιν τὸ πνεῦμα) assumes that a διδόναι τὸ πνεῦμα ἐκ μέτρου would not contradict the nature of the Spirit, though indeed the goodness of God; and Titus 3:6 (οὗ ἐξέχεεν ἐφ' ἡμᾶς πλουσίως) conceives the possibility that the Spirit may also be given sparingly. Expressions such as πνεύματος ἁγίου πλησθῆναι in Luke 1:15,41 and Acts 2:4 and 4:8, or πνεύματος (ἁγίου) πλήρης in Luke 4:1 and Acts 6:3,5 and 7:55 (seldom in the Old Testament: Exod. 28:3; 31:3; 35:31; Deut. 34:9; Mic. 3:8) also appear to originate in the idea that the Holy Spirit fills a person as water fills a container and that as much of the Holy Spirit is given as a person can hold, until he is "full of the Holy Spirit." Indeed, even Rom. 8:23 assumes a partial distribution of the Spirit—Christians have the "first fruits" of the Spirit (partitive genitive).[47] We must note, however, that this is not the prevailing notion in Paul or elsewhere in the New Testament. Rather, the dominant idea is that wherever the Spirit is he is there completely.

Differentiations of Spirit

The Spirit was soon thought of as an abiding, continuously indwelling power that appears on special occasions. The New Testament describes the charismata of the Corinthian community in just this fashion.[48] In Acts 6:5,8 and Luke 2:25 we read καὶ πνεῦμα ἦν ἅγιον ἐπ' αὐτόν (see also, e.g., John 1:32).[49] But the other widespread view is that each single deed of the Spirit follows upon a single and repeated inspiration (see Acts 4:8,31; 7:55; 13:9), a view common to the Old Testament.[50] Both ideas are easy to explain. Sometimes the person's whole demeanor creates such a strange impression that one cannot help but assign the Spirit to him (1 Sam. 10:6, ונהפכת לאיש אחר). Sometimes it is an especially unique occurrence that is so striking it evokes the impression of the divine.[51] Thus Rev. 4:2 presents no difficulties. Eberhard Vischer[52] uses this passage to dispute the unity of the Apocalypse when he writes, "The repetition of the εὐθέως ἐγενόμην ἐν πνεύματι is thoroughly unintelligible, since there is no reason at all why the seer should no longer be in ecstasy." But according to what we have stated above, this expression does not arouse

47. The same idea is clearly illustrated in Tertullian's *Portio Spiritus Sancti:* "apostoli spiritum sanctum habent . . . non ex parte, quod ceteri"; Tertullian *Adv. Marc.* 4. 18; *De exhort. cast.* 4 (from Ritschl, *Altkatholische Kirche,* p. 166, n. 2; p. 481, n. 2).

48. See Heinrici, *Sendschreiben,* p. 393, n. 1.

49. In the Old Testament see, e.g., Gen. 41:38; Num. 11:17; 27:18; Judg. 3:10; 1 Kings 22:24; Isa. 61:1; 42:1; the LXX version of Zeph. 3:4; and Hos. 9:7, in which איש הרוח is translated πνευματοφόρος.

50. Ritschl, *Altkatholische Kirche,* pp. 565–66, offers a parallel from Cyprian.

51. This in contrast to Wendt, *Begriffe,* p. 34.

52. Eberhard Vischer, *Die Offenbarung Johannis: Eine Jüdische Apokalypse in christlicher Bearbeitung* (Leipzig, 1886), in *Texte und Untersuchungen,* vol. 2, fasc. 3.

suspicion at all. The apocalyptist, who up to now has had visions on earth, is about to be taken to heaven (4:2). For this purpose he receives a new bestowal of the Spirit. He is suddenly ἐν πνεύματι again. Further, this utterance has its parallels in En. 71:1,5 and in the Old Testament, for example, in Ezek. 11:1,5, 2:2, 3:24. Generally, the attention of the earliest Christians was directed more toward the sudden, sporadic, and unexpected manifestations of the Spirit (Acts 10:44; 11:15; 8:16: "the Spirit fell . . .").

<h2 style="text-align:center">Symptoms of the Spirit in the
Old Testament and Judaism</h2>

An interesting illustration of the idea that the Spirit is the permanent possession of individual persons is the rather naive tendency in the New Testament age to separate the Spirit of God into various spirits. The differentiation was made by assigning each pneumatic personality its special spirit, no doubt stimulated by the observation that an energy which is similar in individuals still manifests itself in different ways. Since even Paul, who held an entirely different opinion of himself, adopted this differentiation in his usage, we may assume it must have been quite current in his day. (See "the spirit of Elijah" in Luke 1:17, after the fashion of 2 Kings 2:9,15; "the spirit upon Moses" in Num. 11:25; and "the spirits of prophets" in 1 Cor. 14:32). Accordingly, there is absolutely nothing to prevent our construing τὸ πνεῦμά μοῦ in 1 Cor. 14:14 as "the spirit given to me by God." Another differentiation occurs in 1 Cor. 14:12, in which various types of gifts are traced to different spirits (see also 1 John 4:1; 1 Cor. 12:10).

This view of the Spirit and his activities which we have described is not unique to primitive Christianity. It threads its way through the entire Old Testament, was never wholly alien to the Judaism of a later period, and could also count on recognition by the Greeks. So we are justified in calling it the popular view of the New Testament age. We need not spend time proving our first assertion, since it will hardly encounter any opposition. Wendt writes: "In all areas of human activity, natural as well as spiritual, deeds which in their towering ingeniousness and significance exceed the measure of normal human

capacity are traced to the mediation of such a divine רוח."[53]
Everything that betrays a superhuman, enigmatic force that "cannot
be grasped by merely natural presuppositions"[54] is the work of the
רוח. Thus the prophets assert that the רוח יהוה was upon them. They
are convinced that the thoughts pressing in upon them and mightily
moving their inner life cannot be the result of their own reflection and
that the powerful impulse to bear to the people a message that they
cannot resist even if they want to resist is not their own will. "The lion
has roared; who will not fear? The Lord God has spoken; who can but
prophesy?" (Amos 3:8).[55] Job 9:24 gives a characteristic example and
illustrates most clearly why and under what conditions the Hebrew
assumes a divine activity. Job complains that "the earth is given into
the hand of the wicked; he covers the faces of its judges," and in
justification Job adds, "If it is not he, who then is it?" This awesome
faċt that evildoers prevail on the earth, that judges cannot find
justice—from whom does it stem? From God, naturally! אִם־לֹא
אֵפוֹ מִי־הוּא? Thus the Hebrew traces each powerful, awesome,
astonishing event to God. If it is not he, who then is it? It must have
some cause. It is the very same conclusion by which certain
phenomena are perceived as activities of the Spirit of Yahweh. Here
too it is often the unexpected, sudden, and surprising which must be
of divine origin, for example, Samson's sudden deeds of power and
Saul's unexpected and fiery anger—a view that can also be
documented in such robust expressions as פעם צלח (Judg. 13:25),
used of the onset of the Spirit's activity. That first differentiation of
the Spirit which we noted for the New Testament—to the degree our
sources allow us to judge—is only in its beginning stages in the Old
Testament (Num. 11:17; 2 Kings 2:9,15). But it is usual for the Old
Testament to differentiate the Spirit according to the various types of
his activity and thus to speak of a "spirit" of deception, blindness,
somnolence, fornication, wisdom, heroic power, fear of God, and so
on. And the parallel differentiation of the one spirit of life which God

---

53. Wendt, *Begriffe,* p. 32.
54. Ibid., p. 33.
55. See Schultz, *Alttestamentliche Theologie,* p. 217.

gives to all into various spirits or souls begins in the later writings of the Old Testament and is very frequent in the New.

From perhaps the Greek period on, this graphic view of the Spirit altogether recedes in the writings of Judaism, although it is not totally absent. From the Palestinian literature[56] the passages that deserve particular mention are Sir. 48:24, Ps. Sol. 8:15, En. 56:5, 68:2, 71:11, Apoc. Bar. 6, and Bk. Jub. 25, 31, and from the Jewish-Hellenistic literature the statements of Philo regarding inspiration and ecstasy, as well as the words of the Jewish Sybils concerning their inspiration.

We will deal later with those passages in Jewish literature which repeat the hope of the Spirit's outpouring in the messianic age, already spoken of by the prophets, as well as with those which refer to the Spirit without recognizing the ancient, graphic view (The Wisdom of Solomon; Testaments of the Twelve Patriarchs).

The Psalm of Solomon 8:15 speaks of the highly imprudent reception that the Judaean authorities prepared for the Roman general. Rather than keeping Pompey far from the land and the Holy City with all their might, the fools received him as children a father. The result was their ruin. Whence this unbelievable stupidity? God caused it. Because of their sins, ἐκέρασεν αὐτοῖς ὁ θεὸς πνεῦμα πλανήσεως, ἐπότισεν αὐτοὺς ποτήριον οἴνου ἀκράτου εἰς μέθην—a view entirely after the analogy of Isa. 29:10. That which is incomprehensible is effected by a spirit from God. The "spirit of agitation" in En. 56:5 is a perfect analogy to the πνεῦμα πλανήσεως.

In the Apocalypse of Baruch 6, transports in vision are derived from the Spirit *(et ecce subito spiritus fortitudinis sustulit me et extulit me supra murum Jerusalem in altum)*. The same is true of En. 71:5 ("the Spirit translated Enoch to the heaven of heavens") as well as of the Old (Ezek. 2:2; 3:12,14,24; 8:3; 11:1,24; 37:1; 43:5) and the New Testament (Rev. 17:3; 21:10). Here too it is the mysterious effect of power on the human soul which is ascribed to the Spirit.

According to 4 Ezra 14:22, Bk. Jub. 25:3, En. 91:1, 49:4, and 62:3,[57]

---

56. Here and in what follows, the works cited by Schürer in par. 32 of *Die Geschichte des Jüdischen Volkes im Zeitalter Jesu Christi,* pt. 2 (Leipzig, 1886), are reckoned to the Palestinian-Jewish literature.

57. In the Targum of Jonathan, the Holy Spirit is often called the "spirit of prophecy," רוח הנביאה (from Weber, *System,* p.186). So prophecy is here regarded as a characteristic activity of the Spirit.

prophecy and supernatural knowledge—approximately identical in the view of later Judaism[58]—are activities of the Spirit. Particularly in such passages as En. 68:2 ("the power of the Spirit transports and makes me to tremble") and 71:11 ("I cried with a loud voice . . . with the spirit of power") it is clear that the old idea of the Spirit as a superior working, supernatural power of God was not yet forgotten.

Thus the Jewish Sibyl, "the prophetess of the mighty God,"[59] contends that she is the bearer of the ἄψευστον πνεῦμα θεοῦ (3. 701) which "bids" her prophesy (3. 163, 298, 491) and casts on her a spell (ἀνάγκη, 3. 296) from which she vainly prays to be set free (3. 296),[60] and Philo describes the goal of philosophy as attaining to a vision of God in ecstasy: "When the divine madness of prophetic inspiration is to come upon a man, then the sun of consciousness (νοῦς) must be set in him, and human light disappear into the divine. Ecstasy is, therefore, the essential form of prophecy. But this prophecy is not merely reserved for individual, exceptional cases. Every wise and virtuous man is a prophet. He does not speak what is his own, but while his own thought and consciousness have retreated, the divine spirit dwells in him and moves him without his willing as the strings of a musical instrument."[61] Thus Philo himself asserts that he has the Spirit. "Every idea that unexpectedly occurs to him appears to him as an inspiration."[62] And it was particularly his understanding of the hidden sense of Scripture which Philo derived from the Spirit.[63] Perhaps we may ask whether the views of the Sibyl and Philo concerning inspiration derive more from Hellenism than from Judaism. But here too the prophets may have been described as ecstatics to a greater degree than they in fact were. In any case, this idea of the

---

58. See, e.g., Josephus *Antiquities* 13. 10. 7, in which προφητεία equals ἡ τῶν μελλόντων πρόγνωσις. Even in the New Testament. προφητεία and ἀποκάλυψις belong together; see 1 Cor. 14:30.

59. *The Sibylline Oracles: The Apocrypha and Pseudepigrapha of the Old Testament,* ed. R. H. Charles (Oxford: Clarendon Press, 1913), vol. 2, bk. 3, l. 817, p. 393.

60. See Adolf Hilgenfeld, *Die Jüdische Apokalyptik* (Jena, 1857), p. 81: "The manner of this inspiration is thoroughly ecstatic."

61. Eduard Zeller, *Philosophie der Griechen,* 3d ed., pt. 3, sect. 2, 2d half (Leipzig, 1881), p. 415.

62. Ibid., p. 352, n. 1.

63. Ibid.

divine Spirit working suddenly and irresistibly, and to whom—as is especially clear in Philo—is assigned that which appears not to have originated from one's own natural effort, thoroughly corresponds with the Old Testament view. Here then it should be sufficient to indicate that something related to Old Testament ideas appears in pre-Christian, Hellenistic Judaism, whether or not it is to be traced to ethnic influence. And here again it is clear that this view of the Spirit could also be understood by the Hellenes of that period.[64]

The Difference between Old and New Testament
Activities of the Spirit

The concept of an activity of the Spirit, however, is not yet exhausted with the symptoms noted up to now. First of all, a comparison between what the Old and what the New Testament derives from the Spirit indicates that in the New Testament the circumference of the Spirit's activities is considerably smaller. For example, in the New Testament magnificent physical prowess, royal virtue, judicial wisdom, heroic courage, and so on are not assigned to the Spirit and cannot be derived from him. Why not? Because in the Old Testament—I refer above all to the genuinely Israelite period—an event or quality can only be derived from the Spirit of Yahweh which, apart from the peculiar symptoms noted above, is still marked by a connection with the sphere of his power and revelation, with his people. Thus in the Old Testament everything mysterious and mighty in Israel is worked by the Spirit of Yahweh. In the New Testament, by contrast, only appearances that enjoy some relation to the Christian community and its life can be considered pneumatic. That which is mysterious and mighty within the Christian community is "of the Spirit." We can easily see, therefore, that much of what in the Old Testament is regarded as an activity of the רוח seems profane in the New, since it is not even remotely linked to the life of the community. Naturally, what we are referring to here is not a tangible sign, used in the apostolic age for excluding what may not be pneumatic, since it is obviously too indistinct. It is simply characteristic of the concern of the first Christians that the activities of the Spirit in which they

64. See Heinrici, *Sendschreiben*, pp. 350ff., and the passages cited there.

believed somehow had to fall within the sphere of the functions of the Christian community.

The Activities of the Spirit and of Demons

On the other hand, the symptoms noted above would suit the activities of the Spirit as well as those of demons. There is then great similarity between the appearances of demons and the Spirit. This observation is so instructive for an understanding of the concept of Spirit that we must examine it more closely.

From the reproach made of Jesus that he had an unclean spirit, it is clear that a person impelled by the Spirit must in many respects have resembled a demoniac. Although only malicious observers such as the Pharisees pass this judgment (Mark 3:22; Matt. 9:34) or, according to the description of John's Gospel, only such dullards as the Jews (John 7:20; 8:48; 10:20), still, in his pneumatic activity, Jesus must not have been so entirely unlike a demoniac. The judgment that πνεῦμα ἀκάθαρτον ἔχει (Mark 3:30) was not simply nonsense. In precisely the same fashion many of the Jews contended that the Baptist's dark passion came from a demon (Matt. 11:18; Luke 7:33). By contrast, the prehistory in Luke's Gospel regards John as a Spirit-bearer from birth. These observations are strengthened when we consider that the διάκρισις πνευμάτων, or the capacity to distinguish a divine from an unclean spirit,[65] is numbered among the gifts in 1 Cor. 12:10, that Paul intends such discrimination should be rightly used (1 Cor. 14:29), "since even a lying spirit sent from the devil can inspire a man and deceive the church,"[66] and that finally the Corinthians, as is implied in 1 Cor. 12:1-3, had asked the apostle for a positive sign of possession by the Spirit. Even 1 John 4:1-3 responds to such a question, and the manner in which true prophets should be distinguished from false is explained in Matt. 7:15-20, The Shepherd of Hermas, Mandate 2.7ff., and the *Didache* 11. 8ff.[67] since οὐ πᾶς λαλῶν ἐν πνεύματι προφήτης ἐστίν (though indeed, *Didache* 11.7 strongly prohibits cen-

---

65. See Chrysostom, *Hom. ad I Cor. 2:9:* διακρίνειν καὶ εἰδέναι, τίς μὲν ὁ πνεύματι φθεγγόμενος καθαρῷ, τίς δὲ ὁ ἀκαθάρτω.

66. Weiss, *Lehrbuch der biblischen Theologie,* p. 217; see also 2 Cor. 13:3.

67. Ed. Adolf von Harnack in *Texte und Untersuchungen,* vol. 2, no. 1, p. 2 (Leipzig, 1884).

suring a prophet who has already been proved). James 3:15 also distinguishes the wisdom from above from what is demonic. And the warning in Matt. 11:24 and elsewhere against false prophets, to whose enticements one may easily fall prey, indicates that the genuine activity of the Spirit could not be so easily perceived.

This observation is fully confirmed when we compare a few of the statements transmitted to us concerning the activities of the Spirit and of demons.

As does the Spirit, so do the demons have the locus of their activity in the person, through whom, just as the Spirit, they can appear from without.[68]

The activities of the demons applicable here are not at all particularly grievous sins; rather, they are morally indifferent. For the most part, they cause bodily and psychic illnesses. In precisely the same fashion, the manifestations of the Spirit as such do not fall in the moral sphere.[69]

According to the notion of that time, the man who has an unclean spirit is its "house" (Luke 11:24). The pneumatic is the "temple" of the Holy Spirit (1 Cor. 3:16; 6:19). The demon "dwells" in the demoniac (Luke 11:26) and the Spirit "dwells" in the pneumatic (1 Cor. 3:16; Rom. 8:9; 2 Tim. 1:14; see James 4:5). The man attacked by the demon is ἐν πνεύματι ἀκαθάρτῳ (Mark 1:23; 5:2), and the pneumatic is ἐν πνεύματι θεοῦ (Matt. 22:43; 1 Cor. 12:13; Rev. 1:10; 4:2).

The pneumatic utters words of the Spirit—the person is merely the instrument (Rom. 8:15; Gal. 4:6; Acts 21:11; 20:23; Matt. 10:20; 1 Tim. 4:1, etc.). The one possessed utters words of the demon, with whom one can actually converse (Mark 1:34; 5:7ff.). And if the possessed is not accustomed to speaking, then he has a mute, dumb spirit (Mark 9:17,25).

The spirit "cries" out from a person (κράζειν in Rom. 8:15; Gal. 4:6; see En. 71:11 and Ignatius *Phila.* 7: ἐκραύγασα . . . μεγάλη φωνῇ, θεοῦ φωνῇ). In identical fashion the demon cries out from the possessed (κράζειν in Mark 5:5,7; Luke 9:39; Mark 3:11; ἀνακράζειν in

---

68. Mark 5:13 is an exception; see pp. 15–16.
69. See pp. 16–21.

Mark 1:23; Luke 4:33; 8:28; κραυγάζειν in Luke 4:41; βοᾶν in Acts 8:7) and "with a loud voice" (φωνῇ μεγάλῃ in Mark 1:26; 5:7; Luke 4:33; Acts 8:7).

The Spirit can act as an irresistible impulse toward carrying out some deed (see Acts 16:6; 19:21; 20:22) so that the person is "bound" by the Spirit (Acts 20:22).

Thus Jesus is driven by the Spirit into the wilderness (ἄγειν in Luke 4:1, ἐκβάλλειν in Mark 1:12). In exactly the same sense, the demon is said to "seize" (συναρπάζειν in Luke 8:29), to "drive" (ἐλαύνειν in Luke 8:29), to "convulse" (σπαράσσειν in Luke 9:39; Mark 9:20; 1:26), and to "dash down" (ῥήσσειν in Mark 9:18) into the fire, water (Mark 9:22), or wilderness (Luke 8:29) whomever he "binds" (Luke 13:16).

The Spirit can grant superhuman knowledge.[70] But even demoniacs may have a knowledge beyond the natural. One of the surest facts of the gospel history is that the demoniacs first recognized in Jesus the Messiah (Mark 3:12; 5:7; 1:24, etc.; see also Acts 16:17; 19:15; and James 3:15: σοφία δαιμονιώδης).

In some instances the Spirit manifests a miraculous power over nature. We hear also of a demoniac that no chain could hold (Mark 5:4) or are told that those possessed vented their superior physical strength on their exorcists in violent fashion (Acts 19:16).

To have a demon or to rave is often the same thing (John 10:20; see John 7:20; 8:48). Illness of the spirit is the usual effect of an unclean spirit—the counterpart of demonic possession is σωφρονεῖν (Luke 8:35). On the other hand, the Spirit's domination of a person often gives an impression related to madness. To Festus, Paul's "inspired" speech appears as raving (Acts 26:24). The glossolalics provoke the judgment ὅτι μαίνεσθε (1 Cor. 14:23). In Corinth, Paul may have been accused of being beside himself at times (ἐκστῆναι—σωφρονεῖν in 2 Cor. 5:13, just as in Luke 8:35). So, Jesus' relatives anxiously suppose that he is beside himself (Mark 3:21). The case is similar when the Sibyl (3. 816–17) states that if her prophecies should ever come true "no man any more μαινομένην φήσειε, θεοῦ μεγάλην δὲ προφῆτιν."

Whence this manifold agreement? The reason is that in the one as in

70. See p. 35.

the other instance a supernatural power is believed to have taken possession, since the Spirit and the demon are first of all recognized by the same symptoms.

As stated above, the most characteristic activity of the demonic is madness, an illness of the spirit. Whoever is attacked by such an illness is seen to do things that are absurd and unexpected, things that the person by himself would never do. The person is seized by a terrible rage or a deep melancholy that cannot be conceived of as having arisen naturally. Something foreign, not originally his, has penetrated the person. Here and there are observed displays of powerful physical strength which are not assigned to the ordinary person. Such people are also seen to possess a clairvoyance not native to other mortals. Sometimes such phenomena are linked to bodily suffering, the origin of which is not known and the healing of which seems impossible. The entire person gives a sinister impression. Thus, the conclusion is drawn that a supernatural power dwells in him: πνεῦμα ἀκάθαρτον ἔχει.

Those psychic and bodily illnesses were therefore viewed as demonic which made such an enigmatic and powerful impression that there was no wish to assume a natural origin for them. For who else could be their author? אם־לא אפו מי הוא

The way to determine that a person δαιμόνιον ἔχει is thus completely parallel to the way to determine that the πνεῦμα ἅγιον is ἐπ᾽αὐτόν. From the enigmatic and fearful impression of a phenomenon is inferred its supernatural author, conceived as a superhuman power. This explains the manifold agreements among the symptoms of the Spirit's and the demons' sway.

As to the demonic, it should be noted that madness, according to the prevailing, popular opinion of its demonic source, easily assumed special shape, so that even the sick person himself believed he was possessed by demons. Next, we should note that many appearances reported to us in good faith, such as the miraculous knowledge of the demoniacs, are also a mystery to us. We can deny them, but we cannot explain them. But what we cannot explain may still be historical for all that. This also holds true of the "miracles" of the Spirit, of which some will perhaps always remain incomprehensible to us.

This similarity between Spirit and demon is not at all accidental.

Just as did Satan, lord of the demons—in Judaism gradually transformed from a servant of God to his adversary—so the demons themselves emerged from the differentiated, divine Spirit.[71] Though the history of the unclean spirits cannot be as well documented as that of their
prince, the fact itself is not to be doubted. The activities characteristic
of demons in the New Testament, namely, psychic illness, are in the
Old Testament attributed to the divine רוח (1 Sam. 16:14), and the use
of the term התנבא does not distinguish the raving of the one attacked
by madness from the inspiration of the prophet sent from God
(1 Sam. 18:10). First Sam. 10:10ff. and 19:20ff. indicate that in ancient times both phenomena appeared in almost identical form.
"Among the people the prophets were simply called 'raving ones,'
and the term of course was not merely an expression of scorn but quite
common in usage."[72] When in his *Antiquities* (6. 8. 2) Josephus
describes Saul's madness as demonic sickness, he senses quite ap-
propriately that demons and an evil spirit from Yahweh are related
entities. What in ancient times was an evil spirit from God was in
Josephus's day a demon. There is therefore no basis at all for the
contention that in Jesus' day the activities of demons were taken to be
the counteractivity of the infernal kingdom.

As touching the history of demons, it should be noted further that
as early as in the Old Testament other evil spirits appear alongside the
Spirit of Yahweh: "a spirit of harlotry" (Hos. 4:12; 5:4), of
"jealousy" (Num. 5:14,30), a "lying spirit" (1 Kings 22:20–21), an
"unclean spirit" (Zech. 13:2), a "spirit of deep sleep" (Isa. 29:10),
and a "spirit of confusion" (Isa. 19:14). The relationship between
these evil spirits and the demons of a later period is evident.

For an understanding of symptoms of the Spirit, an examination
of that which distinguishes the two entities will be particularly help-
ful, since the manifestations apportioned to each, despite their
similarity, must still have been markedly different. There cannot be
the least doubt of that. Jesus himself calls it an unforgivable sin
to assert that he works in the name of Beelzebub, to declare as satanic

---

71. A similar point is made in Wendt, *Begriffe,* p. 55.
72. Schultz, *Alttestamentliche Theologie,* p. 205. In n. 4 on the same page Schultz
writes: "Note the ancient narrative in 1 Sam. 21:14–16, in which there is an echo of the
awe in the presence of the משגע משתגע."

what in reality is the work of the Holy Spirit (Mark 3:24ff.).

First of all, the demon and the divine Spirit are different in that the latter is assigned much greater power. No demon can open the eyes of the blind (John 10:21). Hence, the more unusual the appearance, the more surely it is caused by the Spirit (see John 9:16,32–33). What is unheard of from all eternity is done by God, not a demon. Indeed, Satan's power is infinitesimal over against the power of God. Even the coming man of sin will do signs and wonders by Satan's power, but the Lord Jesus will slay him with the breath of his mouth (2 Thess. 2:8–9).

Due to the subjectivity of the judgment "This is too great a power for a demon," this distinction between demons and Spirit is of no practical value. It is important only as far as it makes clear the joy of the first Christians at triumphing over the demons by the Spirit's power (see Luke 10:18ff., etc.).[73]

One genuinely distinguishing mark is that the activity of demons is pernicious. The demons cause sufferings and illnesses (κακῶς δαιμονίζεται in Matt. 15:22; κακῶς πάσχει in Matt. 17:15; ὀχλεῖσθαι in Luke 6:18 and Acts 5:16; and καταδυναστεύεσθαι in Acts 10:38). They are themselves "unclean,"[74] do not belong to the "sphere of the divine community,"[75] and appear in contrast to God's Spirit who as such is holy and has absolutely no relation to sin.[76] The demons themselves make known the opposition in which they stand to God and his Son (e.g., Matt. 8:29). The lord of the demons is the devil.[77] Since obviously nothing harmful can come from God, we arrive at the negative definition that everything afflicting the person cannot be an activity of the Spirit. Clearly, this involves first of all what is harmful to man's true salvation. Since the period of the Septuagint (Ps. 96:5;

---

73. A note frequently struck by the apologists; see Harnack, *Lehrbuch,* 1:441.

74. Evidences in Cremer, *Wörterbuch,* p. 453.

75. Ibid.

76. Perhaps we may assume that the designation of God's Spirit as "holy," beginning first with the Old Testament and quite common in the New Testament age, was intended to distinguish him from "unclean spirits." This would explain why this designation emerged only later but then became quite common, for only the later period recognizes "unclean spirits" that have no relation to God, though it too makes frequent reference to them (see the Synoptics).

77. Evidences in Cremer, *Wörterbuch,* p. 244.

106:37; Deut. 32:17; Isa. 65:11), we find that Judaism (En. 19:1; 99:7; Testament of Judah 23; Testament of Naphtali 3; Bk. Jub. 1; 22; Bar. 4:7; Fragment of Theophilus 1.22) identifies the gods of the heathen—whose power over their worshipers could not be denied once they were before one's very eyes—with the δαιμόνια which, because they seduce the heathen to worship, assume a position diametrically opposed to the kingdom of God. But even aside from this, the imaginative view of later Judaism derives every somehow conspicuous sin from an insinuation of demons or of Satan.[78] This view of the activity of the demons, in addition to that noted above, which attributes to them what is morally and religiously indifferent and merely harmful to natural life, is present also in the New Testament (the idol worship of demons in 1 Cor. 10:20–21 and Rev. 9:20). The demons were seen to be either the souls of evil men[79] or the spirits of giants which, according to Genesis 6, the fallen angels had conceived by the daughters of men.[80] It is obvious to Jews and Christians that such enticement to idol worship cannot be ascribed to the Holy Spirit (see Sir. 15:11–12 and James 1:13).

What we can glean from Mark 3:24ff. leads us further. Whoever uses the mighty power that dwells in him—the inference we may draw from this verse—to "heal" (Luke 8:36) the demoniac, to "cure" him (Matt. 17:18; Luke 7:21; 9:42; 13:14; Acts 5:16; 10:38), in him the Spirit of God is at work. And the awful sin of which the Lord speaks in Mark 3:28ff. is that the obdurate man misjudges the blessed dominion of God's Spirit and dares to associate it with Satan intent on ruin. "Only an insolent wickedness, which sins with a rebellious hand, can close the eye to these obviously good works and assign them to a satanic power (!).''[81] This is totally in accord with the fact that to such expressions as "they were frightened" or "they were amazed" the Gospels very often add "they glorified the God of Israel" (Matt. 15:31) or "they glorified God, who had given such authority to men" (e.g., Matt. 9:8; see Mark 2:12; Luke 5:26). This yields a new symp-

---

78. See "Assumptio Mosis" 44–45, in Hilgenfeld, *Messias Judaeorum.*

79. Josephus *Bella Judaeorum* 7. 6. 3: τὰ γὰρ καλούμενα δαιμόνια πονηρῶν ἐστιν ἀνθρώπων πνεύματα; Sib. Or. 3. 547ff., 723; Theophilus Fragment 1. 22; Bk. Jub. 22.

80. En. 15:8ff.; Bk. Jub. 10; Justin *Apology* 1. 5.

81. Ernst Issel, *Der Begriff der Heiligkeit im Neuen Testament* (Leiden, 1887), p. 52.

tom for the activities of the Spirit—their blessing. But this symptom as such applies only to a small number of "spiritual" phenomena and actually only to the healing miracles. Many activities of the Spirit can only later be perceived, or cannot be perceived at all but must be accepted on faith. Conversely, it is conceivable that one may drive out demons and do many wonders in the Lord's name without really "being known to the Lord" (Matt. 7:22; see Mark 9:38).

On the other hand, most spiritual occurrences appear to have been perceived with greater certainty by the fact that they occurred in the name of God or of Jesus Christ or that the name of God or Christ was somehow used.

Here 1 Cor. 12:1–3 is particularly instructive. When the Corinthians ask how pneumatics—and that means glossolalics[82]—may be recognized, Paul answers by reminding his readers of their pre-Christian experience of the demons' power: "One can no more speak in the Spirit of God and say, 'Jesus be cursed,' than he can call him Lord but by the Holy Spirit."[83] It is not man's own doing when he says "Jesus be cursed" or "Jesus is Lord." If he says the first, this shows that he does not speak in the Spirit but that the demons hold sway over him. But if he says, "Jesus is Lord," then it is certain that he speaks in the Spirit, else he would not be able to do so. Now, though the deeper reason for this decision, marked as it is by a truly magnificent optimism, may be specifically Pauline, and though the community may not have dreamed—though Paul's statement allows this inference—of deriving every confession of the Lord from the power of the Spirit who alone makes it possible, it is certainly characteristic of early Christianity that the Christian character of the manifestations of the Spirit is fixed by the symptoms displayed. Whoever speaks of God or Christ speaks ἐν πνεύματι, in the Holy Spirit, for "these are not the sayings of one who has a demon" (John 10:21). The Spirit that cries "Abba!" is God's; the Spirit that praises God, that proclaims τὰ μεγαλεῖα τοῦ θεοῦ (Acts 2:11; 10:46), is sent from God. The power to do miracles in the name of God derives from

---

82. See Heinrici, *Sendschreiben,* p. 359.

83. According to C.F.W. v. Weizsäcker, *Das Neue Testament,* 3d & 4th eds. (Freiburg im Breisgau, 1888).

God. The teacher who proclaims divine mysteries or the prophet who in God's name prophesies concerning God and exhorts to fear of God is inspired by the Holy Spirit. First John 4:1-3 takes the same position. Of course, the theological temper of this statement clearly betrays a later period. Despite that fact, it belongs to early Christianity that it takes its legitimation from the Christian confession of a pneumatic.

This symptom, however, does not apply to everything that in early apostolic opinion was really an activity of the Spirit. It especially does not apply to the extremely significant manifestation of the Spirit by way of an irresistible impulse toward an action with unforeseeable results.[84] And on the other hand, there were and were expected to be false prophets who misuse the name of God so as to deceive the Christians (Matt. 7:15; 24:11; 2 Pet. 2:1; 1 John 4:1; Rev. 2:20). Or there were "false apostles, deceitful workmen, disguising themselves as apostles of Christ" (2 Cor. 11:13)—"and that is not surprising, since Satan himself assumes the mask of an angel of light."[85] So not even this is an unconditionally reliable symptom (see Matt. 7:22).

The only universally valid symptom is that already noted above,[86] namely, that all pneumatic appearances recognized by the earliest community occur only to Christians.

Thus, whoever is convinced of being a child of God has nary a doubt regarding the author of his enigmatic experiences (see, e.g., The Acts of Peter 10:19). This is in accord with the marks given in Matt. 7:16, which are also assumed in the *Didache* 11.8 (οὐ πᾶς ὁ λαλῶν ἐν πνεύματι προφήτης ἐστίν, ἀλλ' ἐὰν ἔχει τοὺς τρόπους κυρίου) and in The Shepherd of Hermas, Mandate 11. 7 (ἀπὸ τῆς ζωῆς δοκίμαζε τὸν ἄν-θρωπον τὸν ἔχοντα τὸ πνεῦμα τὸ θεῖον): ἀπὸ τῶν καρπῶν αὐτῶν ἐπιγνώσεσθε αὐτούς! Practically, this means only that gross immorality such as selfishness, drunkenness, etc. (see, e.g., Rev. 2:20) may not appear in words or deeds that are held to be pneumatic, or in the remainder of a person's life. Of course, armed even with this

84. See p. 33.
85. Second Cor. 11:14, according to Weizsäcker, *Das N.T.;* see also 1 Tim. 4:1.
86. See p. 40.

distinguishing mark, one is subject to error. Who can prove another's Christian character? And yet it is the symptom of an uncommonly great, persuasive power. Here too it finally comes down to the critic's trust in the pneumatic, to the impression made by the pneumatic's entire personality, in many instances raised above suspicion. So we see that the arch-apostles, who at the outset stood aloof from Paul, recognized him "when they saw the grace which was given him." Of course, what is at issue here is neither a mere description of Paul's gospel, which of course was in question, nor a description of his great missionary successes, which may have been nothing but satanic deeds. The decisive factor was rather the pneumatic impression made by the person of Paul which the στύλοι could not avoid, though they may not have wished to take responsibility for his missionary activity.

But if the opinion that "the Holy Spirit prevails in him" is entirely subjective, there is no uncertainty at all as to where it occurs. On the contrary, it is the most awesome sin to confuse the Spirit with a demon. It is a sign of total Pharisaic obduracy to mark down as satanic the pneumatic person of Jesus, precisely in its concretely pneumatic activity, so as to avoid its divine purport. For the Old Testament prophets as well, the first principle on which everything depends and without which their words are altogether vain, is דבר יהוה אשר היה אל פ׳, that is, the recognition of their inspiration, ascertainable only by way of a judgment as to the person.

There is no objectively demonstrable system to prove a revelation divine beyond all contravention. Everything depends on the personal impression, first of all on the impression that an appearance is so enigmatic and powerful that it requires a supernatural author; then, on the feeling that the person by whom it occurs is not unworthy of divine inspiration. This latter conclusion cannot appear so strange when we remember that as early as the apostolic period the gift for recognizing the Spirit was reckoned to be supernatural, a gift of the Spirit not given to every Christian, to say nothing of every person.

Let us summarize our results to this point: Activities of the Spirit are mysterious demonstrations of power in the sphere of human existence which enjoy some kind of connection with the life of the Christian community, which in any event do a person no harm, which often occur by naming the name of God or Christ, and which in all instances concern only such persons who are not unworthy of fellowship with God. The Spirit himself is the supernatural power[87] sent from God through Christ to believers in whom he does great things.

SPIRIT AND MATTER

We must now raise the question as to how the oldest communities conceived the Spirit. As a preliminary question, it has a certain significance for the corresponding question concerning how Paul conceived the Spirit. But we would hardly deal with it if Wendt had not flatly stated that neither the Old nor the New Testament conceived the Spirit as a heavenly or supernatural substance.[88] Since the material from which we must answer our question regarding the apostolic period is very sparse, we will set out this time on another path, and proceed, as Wendt does, from the Old Testament.

Concerning the Old Testament, as soon as we take on the ancient perspective we must be able to see that Hebrew imagination conceived the Spirit of God as a delicate substance, invisible of course to the naked eye though actually present and thus after the analogy of the wind. For the notion of a force without any material substrate requires a highly developed capacity for abstraction which we may not assume the ancient Hebrews had.[89] Indeed, we can say that the more vividly the Spirit's activities are experienced, and the more lively and graphically he is conceived, the more certainly the Spirit will be taken as a supersensuous substance. Usage is and remains the proof for the accuracy of our conjecture.

---

87. Judaism as well as Christianity visualizes the abstract concept of the "supernatural" by contrasting *what exists in heaven above* with *what is present on earth below*. The idea that the Spirit is of supernatural origin is thus expressed in the word that he is sent *from heaven down to* earth; see Matt. 3:16 (καταβαίνειν), Luke 11:13, Acts 2:2, 1 Pet. 1:12.

88. Wendt, *Begriffe,* pp. 34, 50.

89. The same judgment is given in Morris Friedländer, *Sittengeschichte Roms,* 5th ed. (Leipzig, 1881), 3:701: "At that time, the vast majority of people were much less capable than they are now of an abstraction that the concept of a purely spiritual existence requires." This is Friedländer's judgment on the imperial period!

First of all, it is all-important that the Spirit is named after the wind. In order to weaken the inference from this striking analogy, Wendt asserts that the Old Testament conceives of the wind as incorporeal![90] This assertion rests on a fallacy. Since the wind is very often "a figure or expression for what is unsteady, void, and unreal,"[91] it is thought to be viewed as immaterial. If this method of tracing an object from its figure were correct, we would have to conclude that the Hebrews conceived of the wind as unreal, as not actually existing! On the contrary, the wind is merely compared with what is "unsteady, void, and unreal." As Wendt rightly admits,[92] the *tertium comparationis* is "that the wind in its origin and continuance lacks visibility and other marks by which the reality of a thing is usually proved." Hence the wind is compared with what is unreal; it is itself obviously conceived of as existing and as material, namely, as air. That this position is correct is more than adequately proved in Job 37:9, Jer. 10:13, Ps. 135:7 (the "storehouses" of the wind); and Job 28:25 (the "weight" of the wind). It is amply clear from En. 18:1, 34–36, 41:4, 60:11–12, 75:5, 4 Ezra 4:5, 5:37, and Apoc. Bar. 48, 59[93] that Judaism did not hit on the bizarre notion of asserting the immateriality of the wind. And as long as there are warm and cold, dry and moist winds in the world, and as long as the wind still blows in the breeze, the idea will never occur to construe the wind as an immaterial force, for the wind is simply not supersensual.

This fact that the Spirit and wind are compared can be easily explained. Both are mighty in their effects, mysterious in their comings and goings, imperceptible to the human eye, not weighable by human measure, and not to be restrained by human strength. Not only is the Spirit *compared* to the wind, however, but *the same term* is used for both. The conclusion to be drawn from this is that the Hebrew conceived of the Spirit as a kind of wind, more mysterious, more supersensual, perhaps, but nonetheless as a delicate, airy substance. Our assumption has full support in such expressions as נסך, יצק שפך

90. Wendt, *Begriffe*, p. 18.
91. Ibid., p. 19.
92. Ibid.
93. See also Weber, *System*, pp. 198–99.

נשא שים על היה‏, על היה‏, נוח צלח‏, לבש מלא. The "all but accidental emergence"[94] of these expressions does indeed raise something of a problem, but though they describe in various figures the mystery of the descent and possession of the Spirit, they still have in common that they
represent the Spirit as a substance. From these figures we can see that
the Hebrew was not able to conceive the Spirit in total abstraction as a
power without a material substrate. Rather, he had to regard it as in
some sense visible and by conceiving it as a delicate, airy substance.
This is the less surprising as our modern thought, despite all its
capacity for abstraction, immediately envisages every spiritual, independent power as in some sense materially defined. The difference
between modern and ancient thought on this issue is merely that
through our reflection we immediately make clear what is insufficient
in such a view, whereas the ancients, in a naiveté not yet troubled by
reflection, give free reign to their imagination. Further evidences for
this graphic view of the Spirit appear in Num. 11:17,25, 2 Kings
2:9,15, and Ezek. 37:9. The Spirit of life is conceived with special
clarity "as a real breath of God," a concept that Wendt himself
recognizes.[95] So we may assert that wherever the activities of the Spirit
are vividly experienced, the Spirit is visualized as substance. Only
where the Spirit is nothing more than the object of a dogmatic or
religious-philosophical theory (as for example in The Wisdom of
Solomon) does the vivid notion yield to the abstract concept. The first
position may be assumed for Palestinian Judaism in the time of
Christ.[96] Enoch 70:2 actually speaks of the "chariots of the Spirit."
These are the chariots on which Enoch is carried to heaven, just as
Elijah in the Old Testament (2 Kings 2:11). In any event, supersensual
chariots are intended, and indeed, according to 2 Kings 2:11, these
chariots are imagined to consist of fire. Should the translation
"chariots made of spirit" be too realistic, the idea would still be that
the Spirit is most closely linked to an extraterrestrial fire substance
and that this substance is its body, its appearance. The Wisdom of

94. Wendt, *Begriffe,* p. 34.
95. Ibid., p. 21.
96. No proof is needed that in such matters the New Testament authors simply follow
Jewish views. But Wendt (ibid., pp. 20–21) actually derives the New Testament usage
from the Old Testament (!) rather than from Judaism, which he does not consult at all.

Solomon 1:6, 7:7,22ff. gives an abstract, scholarly idea of the Spirit, but even this makes clear (7:22ff.) how uncommonly difficult it was clearly to conceptualize the immaterial without distinctness, even where one strove to do so. In The Wisdom of Solomon the old lively view of the Spirit truly became a desolately barren thought-form.

A series of analogies confirms our assertion. God himself, the angels, the souls of the departed, and in Judaism the heavenly world as well are conceived as in some sense material. It cannot be denied "that the philosophical concept of the spiritual is nowhere to be found in the Old Testament concept of God."[97] Not even the prophets succeeded in "advancing toward the concept of the absolute spirituality of God, however greatly they strove to express the idea of transcendence and immateriality."[98] Enoch 14:20ff., 25:3, 71:10, and Rev. 4:3 indicate the protracted influence of such naive ideas. In exactly the same way, angels are not regarded in the Old Testament as purely spiritual.[99] Of course in Judaism it is said the angels are spiritual essences (En. 15:4,6,7,10), but they are also thought of as able to be bound (En. 10; 69:28; 54:5-6; Bk. Jub. 5:48; Tob. 8:3). First Peter 3:19 refers to $\tau o \hat{\iota} \varsigma \, \dot{\epsilon} \nu \, \varphi \nu \lambda \alpha \kappa \hat{\eta} \, \pi \nu \epsilon \acute{\nu} \mu \alpha \sigma \iota \nu$, which according to the parallels in Enoch must most likely be identified with the fallen angels in Genesis 6 (see Jude 6 and 2 Pet. 2:4). Or the angels are tortured by fire in En. 21:7–10 and 54:67. On the other hand—and this seems to be the prevailing opinion—the angels themselves are thought of as beings consisting of fire and light (En. 71:1 and 2 Cor. 11:14 refer to an $\ddot{\alpha} \gamma \gamma \epsilon \lambda o \varsigma \, \varphi \omega \tau o \varsigma$). For this reason the heavenly world as such is conceived as a realm of light. Even believers shall one day shine as the lights of heaven (En. 104:2; 43:4; 108:13; Dan. 12:3; Apoc. Ezra 7:55; Matt. 13:43). The Apocalypse of Baruch 51 deserves special attention: "Then their splendour [i.e. of the justified] shall be glorified in changes, and the form of their face shall be turned into the light of their beauty, that they may be able to acquire and receive the world which does not die, which is then promised to them. . . . For they shall behold the world which is now invisible to them, And they shall behold the time [$\alpha \dot{\iota} \hat{\omega} \nu \alpha$] which is now hidden from them. . . .

97. Schultz, *Alttestamentliche Theologie,* p. 467.
98. Reuss, *Geschichte,* p. 318.
99. In the modern sense; see Schultz, *Alttestamentliche Theologie,* pp. 559–60.

For in the heights of that world shall they dwell, And they shall be made like unto the angels, And be made equal to the stars.''[100] Here we have a description of the entire upper world, a world of brilliance and light as yet invisible, for the enjoyment of which the earthly and material bodies of the just must be changed.[101] In this world God and the angels live, the latter with a body woven from light, though they cannot yet be seen by human eyes.[102]

These observations are the more valuable because the angels are thought of as spiritual, and because the ideas in Judaism of spirits and angels merge (1 Kings 22:21–22 marks the beginning of such merging). Thus, our inference with respect to the idea of the Spirit is fully justified. Finally, it must still be noted that the Old Testament as well as Judaism conceives even the souls of the dead in שאול as in some sense material. For Judaism, passages such as En. 22:5, 11:27, 103:8, Josephus *Antiquities* 18. 1. 3, and *Bella Judaeorum* 2. 8. 14 furnish the evidence, and in the New Testament the pertinent passages are Rev. 6:9,11 and Luke 24:37.

Taken together, these analogies support our contention that it was obvious to ancient Israelites as well as to Jews—to the extent that Hellenic culture had no influence—that the Spirit is to be construed as material or linked to a material substrate. According to the Jewish view, of course, the substance appears to have been of light.

We have no reason to assume that Jews who became Christians

100. ''Tunc glorificabitur splendor eorum (iustificatorum) in commutationibus, et convertetur figura faciei eorum in lucem decoris eorum, ut possint potiri et accipere mundum qui non moritur, tunc prŏmissus illis. . . . Videbunt enim mundum qui invisibilis est eis nunc, et videbunt tempus (αἰῶνα) quod nunc occultatum est ab eis. . . . In excelsis enim illius mundi habitabunt, et assimilabuntur angelis, et aequabuntur stellis.'' See Charles, Sib. Or., 2. 509.

101. Alongside this idea of the believers' future form of existence, there is another idea in Judaism—belief in a *resurrectio carnis* (2 Macc. 7:11; 14:46). (See Lüdemann, *Anthropologie,* p. 37.) But one has no right to explain the first idea as Hellenistic—though it may perhaps hark back to the quiet influence of Hellenistic ideas—or totally to ignore it (Weiss, *Lehrbuch der biblischen Theologie,* p. 397), since the impulses toward it are attested to in Daniel and Enoch. Both types of ideas have recently been compared by Wilhelm Baldensperger, *Das Selbstbewusstsein Jesu* (Strassburg, 1888). He comes to the somewhat debatable conclusion that the real development of Judaism leads from the ancient prophets' earthbound expectation to transcendental ideas. In any event, up to now there has been enough irritation over the "carnal" hopes of the Jews to allow us to concede the better knowledge that these hopes were actually an inheritance from the prophetic age and that other expectations can also be proved from Judaism.

102. See Apoc. Bar., chap. 51 to end.

abandoned this idea. But it is most worthy of note that our sources, even the Old Testament and Judaism, far from explicitly stating that the Spirit is a light-substance, nevertheless expressly assume this idea—though seldom enough. From this we can clearly see that the chief factor in the concept of the Spirit is always that he is a supernatural power. This is the real definition of the Spirit. The fact that he is conceived as supersensual substance is merely the clothing for a concept that was obvious to the ancients. If in a description of the Old Testament concept of God it would be an error to set out not from Yahweh's power and relation to Israel but from the fact that he is nowhere conceived as purely spiritual, it would be just as great an error to explain the notion of substance as the chief thing in the concept of Spirit.[103]

I have reservations about using terms for the possession and outpouring of the Spirit as proof of the existence of that latter idea in the New Testament. These terms furnish a proof only for the period in which they emerge; in a generation centuries later they may have become "phrases," that is, a fixed way of speaking, the original meaning of which was long forgotten. *Si duo loquuntur idem, non est idem.*

Nevertheless, a quite naive and sensuous view of the Spirit seems to underlie the Pentecost narrative, and the διαμεριζόμεναι γλῶσσαι ὡσεί πυρός are indeed the πνεύματος ἁγίου μερισμός. The word of the Baptist should be included here: "He will baptize you with the Holy Spirit and with fire." It is clear that a sensuous idea of the Spirit appears to emerge from the undoubtedly postapostolic custom of the laying on of hands as well as from the peculiar conferring of the Spirit in John 20:22. Indeed, "how far the limit of the symbolic extends and where the magical begins in conferring the Spirit through the apostles' laying on of hands can hardly be determined from [Acts] 8:17–19 and 9:17."[104] The transfiguration narrative is also of significance for our question. It is to be viewed as an anticipation of the glory of the Lord obtained at the Resurrection (2 Pet. 1:16–17) and clearly shows in what form the exalted Lord was conceived and thus also the hoped-for

103. Thus the statement made by Pfleiderer in *Paulinismus,* p. 199, seems to be somewhat askew.
104. Issel, *Heiligkeit,* p. 64.

future transfiguration of Christians themselves. Through this idea the narrative also witnesses to the nature of the spiritual world above. This harmonizes altogether with what is occasionally assumed of the kingdom of God (see, e.g., Luke 9:27; 13:28; 21:27; 22:16,18,30; Matt. 13:43; 20:21; 25:31). In the matter of naive realism, therefore, oldest Christianity is not at all different from Judaism. In both instances there is need to grasp the objects of religious faith with the understanding but at the same time to conceive them vividly with the imagination. That there is danger in this is clear. These graphic views, originally nothing but the natural expression of religious thought, can become the main topic. They can obviously proliferate and become the object of pseudo-theological reflection. Prophecy thus becomes apocalyptic, in which the traditional ornamentation overshadows the simple, uncluttered truths it was originally supposed to illustrate.[105] Next, life viewed in sensuous-supersensual terms can stifle the sense for the factually given in the past and present and render it useless for practical activity in the world. The Judaism of the Christian period was often subject to these dangers, which were frequently wont to threaten the Christian communities. But an imaginative view as such is not fantastic. Prophecy is not the same as apocalyptic. And this realism in early Christian views is glorious not only because it often contains a wonderful poetry but also and especially because it reveals the unshaken certainty of religious faith during the youth of Christianity—and in a fashion that may put many of us to shame (see, e.g., Matt. 20:21). This realism should not be stunted in exposition. Our observations are confirmed throughout by the visions reported to us. There can be no question that the people of the New Testament believed they saw not images but realities: The glory of God in heaven above and Jesus standing at his right hand (Acts 7:55). Heaven was really opened to them (Matt. 3:16; Acts 7:55) and they really heard God's voice (Matt. 3:17; 17:5)—and at that time the Spirit also became visible. All the narratives of the baptism agree that the descent of the Spirit on Jesus (from the Lord himself or from the Baptist) really took place, though the σωματικῶ εἴδει ὡς περιστεράν in Luke 3:22 may be an error. This is a true indication of the fact that the Spirit

---

105. On the topic see Harnack, *Lehrbuch*, 1:88.

in the early Christian era was more than a concept, an abstraction. The first Christians believed that the Spirit may be visible, though he is naturally withdrawn from ordinary human sight (Apoc. Bar. 51: *detinetur in verbo dei, ne videatur*). But at the same time, they conceived him as material or at least as appearing in a heavenly substance. Mark 5:30 may offer a parallel to this idea of the Spirit (see also Luke 6:19).

THE SIGNIFICANCE OF THE
SPIRIT'S INFLUENCE

It is easy to understand that in the churches highest value was given to all the utterances of the Spirit. God's hand became visible in them. According to Acts, which in this instance is certainly reliable, justification for the mission to the Gentiles was derived from the undeniable fact of the Spirit's outpouring even upon non-Jews (Acts 15:8,12; 11:17; see Gal. 2:9). In particular, words of prophets and glossolalics in the churches could command almost divine authority (see Acts 5:1ff.; 1 Cor. 5:4–5; 1 Tim. 1:20). Indeed, they no longer uttered human words. Τάδε λέγει τὸ πνεῦμα! (Acts 21:11). The mark of this unlimited regard for such spiritual utterances is that they often are described as utterances not of Christian prophets or glossolalics but simply as those of the Spirit. Thus, *in concreto,* "the Spirit expressly says" (1 Tim. 4:1) means "here are some prophecies of some Christian prophets." But the bearer of the revelation is so unimportant that he is not referred to at all (see Rev. 2:7,11,17,29; 22:17; 14:13; Acts 7:51; 20:23; see also Acts 5:3,9, in which a lie to Peter, the Spirit-bearer, is a lie to the Holy Spirit, and putting the apostles to the test means to put to the test the Spirit of the Lord). There are Old Testament parallels in Neh. 9:30, Zech. 7:12, Isa. 63:10, and Hag. 2:5. In Rom. 8:15 and Gal. 4:6 as well, glossolalic utterances are cited as words of the Holy Spirit.[106] (The speech introduced by the διὸ λέγει in Eph. 5:14 is probably the word of a prophet.[107])

106. The words τὸ πνεῦμα λέγει can thus introduce utterances of contemporary prophets as well as words of Holy Scripture (see p. 37). This is characteristic of the regard for prophetic utterances! (See also ὡς θεὸν αὐτὸν ἐκεῖνοι ἡγοῦντο in Lucianus *Peregrinus Proteus* 11.

107. See Harnack, *Lehrbuch,* 1:304, n. 4.

The gifts of the Spirit totally dominated the worship assemblies (1 Cor. 14:26). But the εὔχεσθαι, εὐλογεῖν, and ψάλλειν do not appear to be directly construed as utterances of the Spirit. At least in 1 Cor. 14:15 ordinary prayers uttered τῷ νοΐ are definitely distinguished from pneumatic, that is, glossolalic prayers, and among the gifts of the Spirit enumerated in 1 Cor. 12:8–9,28ff. and Rom. 12:6ff., the gift of prayer is not listed—again proof that every activity edifying the church was not on that account simply taken to be spiritual. As late as in the *Didache,* the prophets who generally "stand at the head of the community" have a special place in the cultus. The pneumatics are "those honored" in the community.[108]

The significance of the activities of the Spirit was of great force for mission. With such wonders Tyre and Sidon would have been converted (Matt. 11:20ff.)! We will not err if we state that the impression they made on Jews and Gentiles was one of the weightiest factors in early Christian propaganda. In 1 Cor. 14:25 we find a prime example of a Gentile conversion. Here the heathen, convicted in his inmost being by the prophets' revelation of all the secrets of his heart, falls on his face and worships God while declaring, "God is really among you!" But the effect on the Jews had to be of even greater significance. Since the end of the Persian era, Judaism no longer possessed gifts of the Spirit. In the Maccabean period they are regarded as long-since past (1 Macc. 9:27). In evidence, Ps. 74:9 and 1 Macc. 9:27, 14:41, 4:46 (see Ezra 2:63; Neh. 7:65) are usually cited; they are passages that assume or lament the absence of prophets.[109] The Talmud contains the very same lament. In the second temple five things were absent: the heavenly fire, the ark of the covenant, the urim and thummim, the anointing oil, and the Holy Spirit.[110] This complaint can be detected in many other lists, the exposition of which is not without value for the New Testament. The gifts of the Spirit can-

---

108. See Harnack's "Prologomena" to the *Didache* in *Texte und Untersuchungen,* vol. 1, no. 2 (1884), p. 131.

109. See the prophecy of Elijah's reappearance in "Malachi," a book that evidently assumes the disappearance of the prophetic spirit at the time of its composition, together with the judgment of Josephus *Contra Apion* 1. 8: διὰ τὸ μὴ γενέσθαι (ἀπὸ δὲ Ἀρταξέρξου μέχρι τοῦ καθ' ἡμᾶς χρόνου) τὴν τῶν προφητῶν ἀκριβῆ διαδοχήν.

110. From Baldensperger, *Selbstbewusstsein,* p. 47.

not have died out completely. This is clear first of all from the fact that the disciples recognized the Lord as the איש הרוח. The idea of the רוח was thus not foreign to them, for these ἄνϑϱωποι ἀγϱάμματοι ϰαί ἰδιῶται (Acts 4:13) certainly did not recognize it from their reading. Still, in Judaism before the time of Jesus the appearances of the Spirit are in full retreat. Not only do we hear nothing of them in the apocryphal, didactic literature or in the historical books (we would have expected, e.g., a prophecy in Tob. 13:14, but instead we read 14:14!) but even in the Jewish apocalypses, which often enough had opportunity, there is surprisingly little reference to the Spirit. As early as from Ezekiel's time it is no longer the Spirit who gives revelation but an angel. Above all, the form of the apocalypses proves our assertion. The authors no longer appear by name as did the ancient prophets. They must borrow the authority needed by a prophetic writing from an ancient man of God, clearly because they did not dare to claim the possession of the Spirit and demand faith in it. They thereby admit they have lost the Spirit and at the same time give witness to the judgment of their contemporaries: "These days, there are no more prophets, no more revelations." What a change from the ancient prophets, who were absolutely certain of their inspiration! How different again the Apocalypse of John (or its Christian editor)! Here the author is expressly named, because he may assume his book will be believed for the sake of his person.[111] In such form the New Testament Apocalypse conforms to the Old Testament prophets. Jewish apocalyptic, on the other hand, conforms to the later pseudo-apostolic prophets—a marked example of the change in the times. Further proof for our contention is that some of the Jewish people who see in Jesus' activity the working of a higher power think he is Elijah or another of the ancient prophets (Luke 9:8). This period appears so spiritually impoverished to them that a man such as Jesus cannot come from it. He is not a child of his time. He must belong to Israel's antiquity, long past and mighty of spirit. Accordingly, the response of John's disciples at Ephesus is entirely credible (Acts 19:2):

---

111. So it is assumed that the author (or editor) of the Apocalypse was called John and by this name was known to the churches. Weizsäcker's opinion (*Zeitalter*, pp. 504–5) that the Apocalypse is pseudepigraphical seems unlikely, since the writing nowhere asserts apostolic origin.

"No, we have never even heard that there is a Holy Spirit." Naturally, they are aware of the existence of the Holy Spirit, but they have not yet learned whether (after the Baptist's death) he is somewhere present and active (see John 7:39). John himself, of course, did not confer the Spirit but merely pointed to the "coming one." But he surely claimed to possess the Spirit—the testimony of the infancy narrative is altogether confirmed by the judgment of his contemporaries in Mark 11:32, and, more significantly, by that of the Lord himself in Matt. 11:9. That he has the Spirit lies in the nature of the case—he appears as προφήτης. He could do so only if the word of God had come to him (Luke 3:2), only if he were convinced he spoke through the Spirit.[112] Thus, to the extent that our sources allow us to judge, John the Baptist is the first since the Persian era to appear in Judea as a prophet and therefore in possession of the Spirit. But this appearance of a pneumatic before Jesus' time is only an isolated case. In Jewish piety, belief in the Spirit had a place only to the degree that the ancient time was held to be inspired and the precious deposit of that inspiration thought to lie in Holy Scripture, and to the degree that there was hope for an outpouring of the Spirit in the messianic age, in accord with the prophetic promises. To the present age, the Chaldeans' statement in Dan. 2:11 applied: The dwelling of the gods "is not with flesh." Indeed, it would be completely absurd on this account to deny to Judaism any vital religiosity. It lacked the original, creative power in the realm of religion, a power prevailing in the prophets' time when "the Spirit of Yahweh was still in Israel," but it did not lack "zeal" for God's cause. On the contrary, we must conceive the time of Christ as most highly aroused in a religious sense—but it still did not have the Spirit!

There are of course isolated traces in Judaism of the Spirit's activities. The Essenes were credited with the gift of prophecy (Josephus *Antiquities* 15. 10. 4–5), and the high priest Hyrcanus is supposed to

---

112. Bernhard Weiss (*Das Leben Jesu,* 2d ed. [Berlin, 1888], vol. 1) expresses this idea emphatically: "Thus we must also admit that John was . . . a prophet in the real sense" (pp. 287–88). But the historical judgment can only be that he claimed to be a prophet. Whether or not he really was cannot be decided by the historian. This judgment is correct only to the extent that John is the only one among the later Jewish prophets to be recognized by Christians after the pattern of their Master.

have possessed it (*Ant.* 13. 10. 7), just as popular Jewish belief attributed προφητεύειν to the high priest of the moment (see John 11:51). Only some time (approximately fifteen years) after the Lord's death, when the Roman authorities, without appreciation for Jewish custom and religion, began to spark the highly inflamed populace to rebellion, did prophets again appear (Theudas under Fadus, see Josephus *Antiquities* 20. 5. 1; Acts 5:36; the Egyptian under Felix, see Josephus *Bella Judaeorum* 2. 13. 5; Acts 21:38; and many others, see *Bella Judaeorum* 2. 13. 4; *Antiquities* 20. 8. 6.). Even at the siege of Jerusalem such prophets played a great role (see *Bella Judaeorum* 6. 5. 2,4).

However ruinous for their people the appearance of these prophets might have been, they do not at all deserve the epithet applied to them by the Romanophile Josephus. They were not deceivers and charlatans but men who in commendable zeal believed in their divine mission and in the imminent establishment of the kingdom of God after all these woes, and they paid for their enthusiasm with their lives.[113] The epithet "deceiver" or "charlatan" belongs to Josephus, who saved his miserable life with trumped-up prophecies (see *Bella Judaeorum* 3. 8. 3,9). Indeed, the frequency of the appearance of these prophets occurs only in the final period before and during the revolt (from approximately A.D. 55 onward). So far as we know, during Jesus' time and in the first two decades of the apostolic age, activities of the Spirit in Judaism could only be identified in highly scattered instances.

If the Jewish opinion[114] that the חכמים received the Spirit in סמיכה (ordination) was widespread among Pharisees at the time of Christ—which to us seems most unlikely—it was in any case a lamentable presumption, for a pneumatic preaches very differently from the scribes. His word is ἐν ἐξουσία (Luke 4:32; Matt. 7:29). And truly, miracles of the Spirit do not arise out of sober study of the Law (see Gal. 3:2).

But what a powerful impression the πνεῦμα must have made when its fullness appeared to a Judaism bereft of the Spirit. Despite that fact,

113. See Adolf Hausrath, *Neutestamentliche Zeitgeschichte,* 3d ed. (Munich, 1879), 1:202–4.
114. Referred to in Weber, *System,* p. 123.

the number of converted Jews must be reckoned as few, which proves how strong the antiprophetic and thus antievangelical tendency in Jesus' time was, a tendency later culminating in the Talmud.

The significance that the manifestations of the Spirit had for the assurance of the Christians, and thus also for their mission, particularly among the Jews, can be fully grasped only when we consider the significance of the gifts of the Spirit for the eschatological hope.

The horizon of the earliest community was in essence eschatological. That the crucified Jesus is the Messiah sent from God who will shortly return to judge all mankind and give his blessed kingdom to his own—this is the chief concept in oldest "Christianity." With Jesus' appearance in the world the great turning point in history has been reached. The time is fulfilled, the first aeon is in its death throes, the end of the world is at hand. A new aeon is approaching in which God reigns, an aeon promised by the prophets. The certainty of this faith, kindled by the unique impression of the person of Jesus, the pneumatic $\kappa\alpha\tau'\,\dot{\epsilon}\xi o\chi\acute{\eta}v$, was daily confirmed by the presence of spiritual gifts which allowed a foretaste of the powers of the world to come. The appearance of the Spirit is a "sign of the times."

The Lord himself regarded the gifts of the Spirit in this fashion.[115] When John relayed to him his famous question (Matt. 11:3ff.) the Lord held back the confession of his messiahship and pointed John to his deeds, which had occurred before all the world. These are the deeds which, according to the promise of the prophets, should occur through the Messiah in the last time. From them John may see who Jesus is—the bearer of the Spirit, the Messiah. Jesus' miracles are thus not a legitimation of his divine mission as such but the proof of his messiahship.

When we observe, however, that the Lord's answer contains no real reference to a prophetic passage, and that it is only loosely linked to a few utterances from Isaiah (Isa. 61:1; 35:5ff.), then in order to understand the rigor of the inference that he draws we must assume a closer connection between the concepts "Messiah" and "Spirit," a connection inherent in the nature of the case. The Lord clearly assumes this connection in somewhat different form: "But if it is by

115. This is of great significance for understanding Jesus' self-consciousness, a factor that Baldensperger has overlooked in his description of Jesus' self-consciousness.

the Spirit of God that I cast out demons, then the kingdom of God has come upon you" (Matt. 12:28). If Jesus can act in the Spirit of God, then the kingdom of God is at hand. "Where the Spirit is, there is the kingdom of God"—this is his assumption. The appearance of the Spirit is the breaking in of a new age in which the kingdom of God is coming. If Jesus acts in the Spirit—and this, he contends, no one can deny—then the kingdom of God is nigh! The powers of the new world have appeared in the midst of the old—Ἰδοὺ ἡ βασιλεία τοῦ θεοῦ ἐντός ὑμῶν ἐστίν!

This link between the Spirit and the kingdom of God requires explanation. In the New Testament this link appears only in Rom. 14:17, and not even there as directly as in our passage. (The relation between the two concepts explains their alternation in the variant readings of Luke 11:2.) In contrast, the "kingdom of God" and the "power of God" are often juxtaposed. The kingdom of God comes ἐν δυνάμει (Mark 9:1); it consists ἐν δυνάμει (1 Cor. 4:20), just as it is said that the Son of man will return upon the clouds μετὰ δυνάμεως πολλῆς καὶ δόξης (Mark 13:26; Luke 21:27; Matt. 24:30; see Rev. 12:10: ἄρτι ἐγένετο ἡ σωτηρία καὶ ἡ δύναμις καὶ ἡ βασιλεία τοῦ θεοῦ ἡμῶν, and the inauthentic doxology of the Lord's Prayer in Matt. 6:13).

Every kingdom exists so long as there is a power to preserve it. And the kingdom of God, which is "that order of things in which the validity of the divine will is manifest,"[116] is in a quite special sense inconceivable apart from power. For the kingdom of God is in opposition to all the kingdoms and powers of this age, especially the kingdom of the devil. The coming of the kingdom of God is therefore an act of God's supernatural power. And conversely, wherever the transcendent power of God is manifest, wherever the Spirit of God enters to break the devil's might, there is the kingdom of God. "So from the very beginning it was these mighty deeds of Jesus which became a shining witness to his peculiar calling."[117] Jesus' mighty deeds revealed the presence of the Spirit, the kingdom of the Messiah. This enables us to understand why Jesus linked his σημεῖα to his preaching and also commissioned and authorized his disciples to do them, for the activities of the Spirit, in the power of word and deed, are the legitimation of the gospel.

116. Cremer, Wörterbuch, p. 192.
117. Weiss, Leben Jesu, 1:444.

In the New Testament writings there are similar and again fairly frequent references to indicate how much the faith of the earliest community was supported by the activities of the Spirit. These activities are the persistent witness to Christian faith.

Thus Peter's Pentecost sermon refers to the passage in Joel (3:1ff.; LXX: 2:28ff.). The event that the prophet announced should take place ἐν ἐσχάταις ἡμέραις has now occurred.[118] The "promise of the Holy Spirit" (Acts 2:33) is fulfilled. But it is upon Jesus' disciples that the Spirit has descended: "Let all the house of Israel therefore know assuredly that God has made him both Lord and Christ, this Jesus whom you crucified." The outpouring of the Spirit is the fact, the messiahship of Jesus the consequence, and the fulfillment of prophecies the proof.

When Heb. 6:5 states that the Christians have tasted the powers of the age to come (a similar expression occurs in Barn. 1:7: τῶν μελλόντων δοὺς ἀπαρχὰς ἡμῖν γεύσεως) and also views the mighty deeds of God's Spirit as a penetration of the present by the coming age, it suggests an inference that is actually drawn in Heb. 2:3ff.: "Salvation, first begun through the preaching of the Lord, and attested to us by those who heard him, accompanied by God's witness in signs and wonders and various powers and distributions of the Holy Spirit, according to his will. For not to angels has he subjected the world to come, of which we are speaking."[119] Through the activities of the Spirit, God makes it known that he desires to give us the world to come, since the Spirit is the δύναμις μέλλοντος αἰῶνος. Here too the legitimation that God gives the apostles does not rest with their speaking by divine commission. Rather, God witnesses to the reality of salvation and thus to the content of their preaching by joining to it a constituent of salvation—the outpouring of the Spirit.

One of these evidences is cited when in Acts 5:32, together with the disciples themselves, the Holy Spirit given by God witnesses to the exaltation of the crucified One, or when in Acts 14:3 the Lord himself witnessed to the word of his grace by allowing signs and wonders to

---

118. It is interesting to note that the author of the speech characteristically alters the words ἐν ἐσχάταις ἡμέραις (in the LXX, μετὰ ταῦτα; and in the Hebrew, אחרי כן), and thus quite correctly grasped the prophet's intent. That he did so indicates how he valued the reference to time.

119. According to Weizsäcker's translation.

occur through his disciples' hands. Thus for each individual the Spirit is a witness from God that he is a believer, and that God desires to give him salvation (Acts 15:8; 10:47). We may assume the presence of similar ideas in 1 Pet. 1:2: the Christians are ἐκλεκτοὶ παρεπίδημοι . . . ἐν ἁγιασμῷ πνεύματος, and in 1:12: οἱ εὐαγγελισάμενοι ὑμᾶς ἐν πνεύματι ἁγίῳ ἀποσταλέντι ἀπ᾽ οὐρανῶν. In both instances the dominion of the Spirit is accented because it is a divine legitimation for the reality of the Christian profession (1 Pet. 1:2) and for the truth of the apostolic preaching (1 Pet. 1:12). But it is assumed that we know why the Spirit should be this witness.

Indeed, from the passages cited we gain no clear impression of the vitality of these perceptions of the Spirit in the community or of the value assigned the activities of the Spirit. The reason is that Acts, which is first to lead us to these questions, yields an already faded picture from which the original colors scarcely shine through. Paul gives us a much better orientation to the spiritual gifts of the early communities, and his statements will confirm what we have said above.

THE DANGER INHERENT IN THE
APOSTOLIC VIEW

The danger in the apostolic view of the Spirit cannot be ignored. Bearers of the Spirit who could not be controlled with any certainty and who themselves enjoyed the highest esteem could indeed speak as the revealers of God—what could result from such an authorization! Christianity as a historical religion could be lost.[120] In the subsequent course of history, what actually has not been advocated as Christian on the ground of a vaunted possession of the Spirit! One of the great accomplishments of divine providence is that the church has survived this danger. And what has saved the church? Not a pneumatic speculation such as Paul's, which could offer no assurance of keeping to the path of the historically given gospel. It was rather the infinitely powerful impression of the historical Jesus which prevented Christendom from forfeiting its historical character. In this respect the remembrance of Jesus paralyzed the pneumatic phenomenon of the apostolic age and it still survives after more than a thousand years.

120. Another danger in the gifts of the Spirit is discussed on pp. 85–90—the disruption of the life of the community by enthusiasm.

2

THE TEACHING of PAul

To the extent dealt with in recent monographs, Paul's teaching is almost always discussed in relation to his doctrine of the flesh. Naturally, for Paul these two concepts are so related that it is impossible completely to ignore the one while discussing the other. But it is another question whether it is proper in investigation to set out from this contrast, or, to begin with at least, to taper the investigation in the direction of such a comparison. This procedure can be fatal, especially for our question regarding the teaching concerning the πνεῦμα. For, since what seems to be at issue in the Pauline relation between flesh and spirit is first of all a relation between two concepts, it is tempting to conceive of the Spirit in Paul as a "concept" that merely needs defining in order to be mastered. But to this concept belong very concrete views and deep inner experiences in which we must imitate the apostle in order to understand his dogmatic statements. The apostle's vital conviction regarding the πνεῦμα is not at all exhausted with a proper definition of the concept of Spirit. And it is not merely the task of New Testament theology to transmit correctly and in topical sequence the available utterances of the New Testament authors. The theologian's far more difficult and attractive duty is to understand these authors from out of their own views and experiences.[1] Obviously this is particularly necessary over against an author

1. See Otto Pfleiderer, *Paulinismus* (Leipzig, 1873), pp. iv ff. I thus totally agree with J. Gloël's exposition (*Der heilige Geist in der Heilsverkündigung des Paulus* [Halle, 1888], p. 369) and am pleased to see he has ventured to write 368 pages on the Spirit in Paul before first attempting a real definition (pp. 369ff.). I am convinced that biblical theology is the greater advanced the more we become aware that the New Testament has to do with living views and not with sharply delineated doctrinal definitions.

such as Paul, whose primary concern is not at all theoretical and dialectic but rather practical and religious.[2]

Since Carl Holsten's investigations the question has often been raised as to which sources are to be used to explain and evaluate the Pauline thought forms. A direct tie with the Old Testament would scarcely suit an author who always views Holy Scripture in more or less allegorical fashion. It is a grave error in method, which must result in a mass of misconceptions, to attempt to derive Paul's sphere of ideas or even his usage directly from the Old Testament and consequently to ignore the apostle's origin in Judaism. The question can only be, Is Paul dependent on Palestinian or Hellenistic Judaism or is he not? We cannot answer this question from our knowledge of the apostle's life. Paul is a Jew of the Diaspora, but he was educated in Jerusalem. Still, there were also Hellenists in Jerusalem, and his later conversations with Greek-educated Jews and Hellenes may have influenced him. So this question cannot be decided a priori. Hence, we first must disregard every such attempt at a connection. This method has special significance to the extent that the concept of the πνεῦμα is linked to that of the σάρξ. For a description of Paul's teaching concerning the πνεῦμα, however, another connection is allowed, even needed. We have seen that Paul was aware of the ideas concerning the πνεῦμα which were prevalent in the churches. We will have to test whether he approves them and whether on this basis an understanding of his own teaching is to be gained.

PAUL'S PRACTICAL POSITION TOWARD GIFTS OF THE SPIRIT

We will not describe Paul's dogmatic theories concerning the Spirit now, but we will, at the outset, raise this question: What practical position did Paul assume toward what the opinion of the Christian churches conveyed to him as pneumatic? We believe that by putting this point first we can also trace the formation of the ideas of an apostle who was first of all a Christian and then an apostle, who was

2. See Hermann Lüdemann, *Anthropologie des Apostels Paulus* (Kiel, 1872), p. 110, n. 2.

an apostle because he was a Christian (2 Cor. 4:13) and only then felt the need to gain clarity through reflection respecting his conviction.

The answer to our question is obvious—Paul simply acknowledged it all as pneumatic.

Paul himself was a pneumatic to an exceptionally high degree. He had become a Christian through a pneumatic experience, and just as at his conversion he felt God's creative power and had a sense of being seized by Christ (2 Cor. 4:6; Phil. 3:12), so he continually felt a higher hand resting on him. He united almost all the gifts of the Spirit in one person. He ventures to appear in the Corinthian community with a revelation or knowledge or prophecy or teaching (1 Cor. 14:6), and his writings confirm this throughout (for his prophecies, see, e.g., Rom. 11:25 and 1 Cor. 15:51-52). To the Corinthians he can say, "I speak in tongues more than you all" (1 Cor. 14:18). He can tell of visions and revelations in which he was caught up to the third heaven or paradise and heard things that cannot be told (2 Cor. 12:2,4). Indeed, the Lord himself speaks with him and comforts him in his sufferings (2 Cor. 12:9; see Acts 18:9 and 22:17ff.). The Corinthians need not be ashamed of their apostle; he is not at all inferior to the "superlative apostles" (2 Cor. 12:11). He has done among them the signs, wonders, and mighty works that legitimize an apostle (2 Cor. 12:12). His preaching is pneumatic. Christ speaks in him (2 Cor. 13:3). He has the same spirit of faith as the psalmist (Ps. 115:1, LXX): "I believed, and so I spoke" (2 Cor. 4:13). His preaching consists in the demonstration of the Spirit and of power (1 Cor. 2:4; see 1 Thess. 1:5). His own judgment concerning his entire apostolic activity to this moment is: "Christ has wrought through me to win obedience from the Gentiles, by word and deed, by the power of signs and wonders, by the power of the Holy Spirit" (Rom. 15:18-19).

But now, how did this man evaluate the pneumatic gifts given him by God? He is far from disparaging them. On the contrary, just as the communities of his time, he held them to be the most glorious and wondrous gifts of God. And he even sees in them the direct influences of the divine. But as greatly as he rejoices over these miraculous powers, he is still humbly conscious that they are gifts of grace, χαρίσματα, and not his own deeds (see esp. 2 Cor. 12:5,9-10; 4:7).

For the charisma of glossolalia so richly given him, Paul also gives thanks to God (1 Cor. 14:18). His visions and revelations are a highly prized experience. He boasts of them when forced to it (2 Cor. 12:1), and he is conscious that in their abundance lurks the danger of presumption (2 Cor. 12:7). His entire reluctance to speak of these secret revelations indicates that for him they were a sanctuary profaned when spoken of.[3] "These are the conditions and experiences from which he draws his strength, not merely for individual decisions, but for the confidence with which he announces the higher heavenly world and demands a turning toward it."[4]

Paul is joyfully aware of his special grace, his apostleship, this divine "treasure" (Rom. 15:15–16; 2 Cor. 4:7), and against all attacks upon it, in proud confidence, he hurls the word: Paul, an apostle—not from men nor through man, but through Jesus Christ and God the Father! Accordingly, he gently but resolutely claims the authority due an apostle, even over against a strange community (Rom. 15:14ff., 29; 1:1–5,11).

It is particularly surprising that this man, who could render such sober practical judgment when needed, at strategic points in his life allowed himself to be guided not by rational reflection but by revelations and impulses of the Spirit (Gal. 2:2; Acts 16:9).[5]

For Paul the Spirit is also the source of his teaching. When he gives the churches instructions concerning their moral behavior, he states that he thinks he also has the Spirit of God (1 Cor. 7:40; see 1 Clement 47.3), and the wisdom which he also can impart among the mature is a wisdom from God, decreed by God before the ages, hidden until now, revealed through the Spirit, imparted in words taught by the Spirit (1 Cor. 2:7,10,13).

In addition, Paul's understanding of Scripture was pneumatic,[6] and it is precisely those authentically allegorical interpretations of Scripture which will have been particularly convincing for him. We can see this in the confidence with which he presents an argument such as that in Gal. 4:21ff., and when Hermann Lüdemann[7] supposes

---

3. See C.F.W. v. Weizsäcker, *Das apostolische Zeitalter* (Freiburg im Breisgau, 1888), p. 325.
4. See ibid.
5. See ibid.
6. Ibid., p. 582.
7. Lüdemann, *Anthropologie*, p. 184.

"those contrived scripture proofs give him no feeling of certainty," this is absolutely not true of Paul the pneumatic.[8] (Incidentally, see what was said on p. 47 regarding Philo's interpretation of Scripture.)

This makes it clear that Paul had a most vivid view of the πνεῦμα, which he daily felt at work within him, that he assigned to the Spirit the same activities as did the communities near him, and that he thus perceived the Spirit by the same symptoms and evaluated them just as they did. If we were to define the concept of Spirit in Paul, we could do so after the analogy of his own words: δύναμις οὐ τοῦ αἰῶνος τούτου (1 Cor. 2:6), ἥν ἐξαπέστειλεν ὁ θεὸς εἰς τὰς καρδίας ἡμῶν. First of all, then, we regard as the essential component of this concept in Paul that the Spirit is an absolutely supernatural, divine power. Next, that it is characteristic of this power to find the place of its activity in a person's heart. Through the first, the Spirit is distinguished from all natural powers; through the second, from other factors related to the divine. This serves as a preliminary orientation.

It is obvious, therefore, that this man, for whom the Spirit was everything, thoroughly recognized and valued the pneumatic in others wherever he met it.

Of particular interest to us are two passages dealing with the witness of the Holy Spirit. The Spirit cries, "Abba! Father!" (Gal. 4:6), or (Rom. 8:15) in the Spirit we cry, "Abba! Father!" For Paul, this cry in the Spirit is proof that the Christians are truly children of God. Indeed, the Spirit himself bears witness to it (Rom. 8:16). At issue here must be a cry that was heard often enough among Christians—Paul assumes acquaintance with it in Rome and Galatia—and was conceived not as the cry of those who uttered it but as the word of the Spirit himself. This follows particularly from Rom. 8:16,[9] and the basis for proof is in both passages. This crying of the Spirit is a heavenly guarantee of the status of Christians as children. The apostle and his readers are absolutely certain that it is really an utterance of the Spirit—it needs no proof. So it is not inferred from their content

8. Adolf von Harnack's judgment on the Montanists (*Lehrbuch der Dogmengeschichte,* 2d ed. [Freiburg im Breisgau, 1888], 1:385–86) applies also to Paul: "These Christians *still* knew *nothing* of the absoluteness of an historically *concluded* revelation of Christ as the basic condition of Christian consciousness." Indeed, this is not so much characteristic of Paul himself as of his entire age.

9. In our opinion, v. 16 *interprets* the preceding ἐν ᾧ κράζομεν· ᾿Αββᾶ ὁ πατήρ. Gloël is of another opinion (*Der heilige Geist,* pp. 200ff.).

that these words could only be understood as a cry of the Spirit.[10] Rather, Paul concludes from their Spirit-wrought character that the content of these words must be true. That means that these words must belong to prayers marked by such symptoms that their suprahuman origin had to be immediately recognized, that is, as prayers uttered in ecstasy, in which not the person but rather τὸ πνεῦμα προσεύχεται (1 Cor. 14:14).[11] The term κράζειν also supports this contention (see En. 71:11; Ignatius *Phila.* 7). Hence, what must be involved here is glossolalia or something similar,[12] and it is of greatest concern to note that Paul acknowledges glossolalic utterances without hesitation and in his arguments uses them alongside other witnesses.[13] So it is not at all to be assumed that the words "Abba! Father!" are thought of as the opening lines of the Lord's Prayer. It is another question whether the frequent cry "Abba!" can be interpreted through the influence of the Lord's Prayer, as Weizsäcker supposes.[14] The latter also seems unlikely to me, since according to oldest tradition (Matt. 6:9) the Lord's Prayer began with a πάτερ ἡμῶν, which is the equivalent of אבונא, and not אבא (as in Luke 11:2: πάτερ).

Similarly, Rom. 8:26 speaks of a sighing of the Spirit, which, as the groaning of creation (vv. 19–22) or of Christians (vv. 23–25), guarantees a future glory (v. 18).[15] There can be no doubt as to what Paul intends by the Spirit's sighs that are too deep for words. They are uttered by the Christian in a condition in which he is no longer able clearly to express the feelings which powerfully seize him but pours them out in sighs, "whose meaning words cannot express." Now, these sighs are conceived no longer as the product of some human

---

10. This idea, inserted by Gloël (ibid., p. 196), is completely lacking in Paul.

11. According to this it is obviously an error when Harnack (*Lehrbuch,* 1:47, n. 1) distinguishes "the Spirit through whom we cry: 'Abba, dear Father,' from the 'spirit of ecstasy' in Paul."

12. Whether these explanations—all but identical with the definition Paul gives of glossolalia in 1 Cor. 14—thoroughly coincide with the phenomena assumed here is a question of secondary importance.

13. Tertullian uses the utterances of the Paraclete as divine authority in exactly the same way; see Gottlieb N. Bonwetsch, *Montanismus* (Erlangen, 1881), p. 17.

14. Weizsäcker, *Zeitalter,* p. 577.

15. The sequence of thought according to Bernhard Weiss, *Der Brief an die Römer,* in H.A.W. Meyer's *Kritisch exegetischer Kommentar über das Neue Testament* (Göttingen, 1881), p. 371.

activity of soul but as the sighs of the Spirit himself. They are therefore glossolalic-ecstatic outbursts which, because they are expressed by the Spirit himself, are used by Paul as an objectively valid proof for the reality of the blessing of salvation. These observations are all the more interesting since the very same Paul, as is well known, did not place particularly high value on glossolalia in relation to the other gifts. But it never occurred to him not to construe glossolalia as pneumatic. Here we see most clearly that in his understanding and evaluation of the gifts of the Spirit, Paul entirely agrees with the judgment of the earliest Christians.

In other contexts as well the presence and activity of the Spirit in the world are for Paul a divine guarantee of the Christian faith. First of all, he reminds the foolish Galatians—and by this it is his intention to give conclusive proof for the divine origin of his gospel—of the mighty deeds that have occurred among them (3:1-5). These deeds are witnesses from God, so clear, indeed so palpable, that even a blind man (v. 1) must see them (τὸ πνεῦμα in v. 2 is interpreted by v. 4; and the Galatians will have assumed an advance in Christian life from works of the Law). Did these miraculous occurrences teach them nothing? Did they have such glorious experiences in vain?

For Paul, just as for the primitive Christian community, the understanding of the spiritual gifts as guarantee for the truth of the gospel has an eschatological apex. Indeed, those activities of the Spirit which Paul views as such are not simply those that the churches of the apostolic age derived from the Spirit. But we can first of all ignore what is common to Paul and his age, and must later deal with the eschatological significance of the Spirit. At any rate, Paul and his age agree in the conviction that the Spirit is present, at work among Christians, and that the fact of his presence proves the truth of the "gospel."

Of course, the idea that the gifts of the Spirit, because they were predicted by the prophets, prove that the words of the ancient men of God concerning the last times are now beginning to come true, is not found in Paul. Only Eph. 1:13 seems to refer to this idea (τῷ πνεύματι τῆς ἐπαγγελίας). Paul merely asserts that the Holy Spirit now given the Christians is the content of that promise God once gave Abraham (Gal. 3:14). It is important to recognize that in the same context (Gal.

3:18,29) the κληρονομία or inheritance of the eternal future kingdom (κληρονομεῖν βασιλείαν, Gal. 5:21) appears as the essential content of the divine ἐπαγγελία (see Rom. 4:13). Thus for Paul the present possession of the Spirit and the future possession of the kingdom are so mutually related that they can be interchanged. Let us examine what constitutes the relation between these two saving benefits. In Rom. 8:23 the apostle describes the present possession of the Spirit as an ἀπαρχὴ τοῦ πνεύματος, which guarantees a future and total possession. The assumption, therefore, is that the Spirit is the present and future possession of Christians—partial conferral in the present guarantees complete bestowal in the future.[16] The other idea is more frequently expressed, namely, that Christians already possess the Spirit entire, and for this very reason they can believe God will give them the kingdom at the appearing of his Son. The Spirit is the seal by which God has marked those who are to share his promises (2 Cor. 1:20) and his heavenly kingdom (on v. 22, see Eph. 4:30; on the idea as such, see Rev. 7:3, following Ezek. 9:4). He is the earnest who is to guarantee a future, total payment still outstanding (2 Cor. 1:22; 5:5; see Eph. 1:14). Precisely because of this possession of the Spirit, the individual Christian is certain he also is destined for a share in the future kingdom. Paul is convinced of the Thessalonians' election because he was permitted to preach among them in power and in the Holy Spirit and with full conviction—that the Spirit aided him at Thessalonica with his power proves that God intended to establish a community there—and because, despite much affliction, they received the word with joy inspired by the Holy Spirit (1 Thess. 1:4-6). In Corinth the witness to Christ is confirmed through the richness of grace poured out on the community, "so that you are not lacking in any spiritual gift, as you wait for the revealing of our Lord Jesus Christ" (1 Cor. 1:7).

Paul is therefore convinced that Christians, precisely because they have received the Spirit from God, can be certain he will also give them a share in the heavenly inheritance. So for Paul there must be an

16. The above remark applies even if the πνεύματος in v. 23 should be a partitive genitive—an assumption, however, which is not fully certain. It would be just as appropriate to conceive it as an epexegetical genitive, as Gloël prefers (*Der heilige Geist,* p. 207).

inner connection between the concepts πνεῦμα and βασιλεία τοῦ ϑεοῦ.

Romans 8:15-17 and Gal. 4:6, however, do not offer sufficient explanation for these sequences of ideas. The thought here, that certain utterances of the Spirit confirm the sonship of Christians with God and thus also their future κληρονομία, contrasts with the thought noted above, according to which the fact of the Spirit's outpouring as such assures the Christians of the final fulfillment. The two ideas may thus not be reduced to one. We can only understand the confidence in these conclusions when we first consider that for Paul as well the powers which he perceives in himself and his communities do not derive from this aeon (1 Cor. 2:6-7)—they are much too mighty for that (2 Cor. 10:4-5)—but witness to the presence of something supernatural: the power of God's kingdom (1 Cor. 4:20) already filling Christians now. Of course, for Paul as well as for the synoptic Gospels the kingdom of God is "the messianic kingdom whose establishment enters with the parousia in the αἰὼν μέλλων."[17] But in the midst of this world the powers of the future world are already manifest. The future kingdom penetrates this world in advance (1 Cor. 4:20). The blessing given to Christians is righteousness and peace and joy in the Holy Spirit, in which that very kingdom consists (Rom. 14:17). Πνεῦμα and κληρονομία therefore belong together—the former is the present, the latter the future participation of Christians in the kingdom of God. He who gave the one will certainly give the other. He who has begun will also complete. God is faithful.

Paul frequently expresses this connection between the present possession of the Christians and their future inheritance in another way. The Spirit is also "the power of supernatural life in the heavenly state of existence."[18] Christians, who already have the Spirit, can trust that God, for the sake of the Spirit which dwells in them, will also give life to their mortal bodies (Rom. 8:11). Thus, the present activities of the Spirit guarantee still another activity of that Spirit in the future. We will amplify this idea later when we deal with what is specifically Pauline. But here we must determine whether the idea as such is peculiar to the apostle. It is only Paul who infers from a present pos-

17. See Weiss, *Römer,* on Rom. 14:16.
18. H.H. Wendt, *Die Begriffe Fleisch und Geist* (Gotha, 1878), p. 147.

session of the Spirit that the Spirit will bring about eternal life. This is not true of the idea underlying this inference, namely, that of the Spirit as the power of supernatural life. The idea is obviously foreign to the Old Testament (in Dan. 12:2 there is no reference to the Spirit), but it does appear to have been common to later Judaism (see 2 Macc. 7:23; Syb. Or. 4. 187; Rev. 11:11: πνεῦμα ζωῆς). And this opinion is only a natural outgrowth of Old Testament ideas[19] attested to in Judaism (see, e.g., Jth. 16:14; Apoc. Bar. 3, 23, 85; 4 Ezra 3:5; 6:39; Syb. Or. 4. 46,187; Assumption of Moses 44) and in the New Testament.[20] The Spirit as a continually active power is life—for the Hebrew, ideas in parallel are lively and highly effective— and all life in the world, all this mysteriously active force, is conceived as a dispensation of the Spirit. Thus, where there is hope in a new existence beyond this life it is obviously conceived as worked by the Spirit of God (see the allegory in Ezek. 37). But especially a life that is absolutely supernatural can rest only on the power of the Spirit. So also for Paul it is obvious that the Spirit gives life (2 Cor. 3:6; 1 Cor. 15:45; Rom. 8:2; see also Apoc. Bar. 23: *spiritus enim meus creator vitae est*). Whoever has the Spirit cannot die.[21] And the Spirit's activity in the person is the guarantee of eternal life.[22]

This helps us understand that for Paul possession of the Spirit was one of the surest signs of the imminence of the divine kingdom. Of course, Paul always assumes the distinctive mark of the eschatological hope, namely, that the kingdom of heaven is nigh, always ahead. He is never forced to prove it expressly because for him and his time, being a Christian and "waiting for the Lord" are identical. But when, following the impression given us by Paul's letters, we inquire as to the basis for his conviction that "the ends of the ages have come upon us" (1 Cor. 10:11)[23] or that "the form of this world is passing away"

19. Evidences in ibid. pp. 21–22.

20. The passages in ibid., p. 46.

21. See Bernhard Weiss, *Lehrbuch der biblischen Theologie des Neuen Testaments,* 4th ed. (Berlin, 1884), p. 394.

22. Here then the Spirit is to be conceived as a power transforming persons from within, not as influencing human nature from without. See Gloël, *Der Heilige Geist,* p. 379. This confirms our observation on p. 15.

23. According to C.F. Georg Heinrici (*Das erste Sendschreiben des Apostels Paulus an die Korinther* [Berlin, 1880]) on the passage.

(1 Cor. 7:31) and a new one approaching, then we can confidently reply that this conviction rests on his pneumatic experiences. First of all, they furnish him evidence of the reality of a higher world. That he can trace the powers of that world in himself, now, in the present, proves that the end is near, since Paul and his age view the opposition between the pneumatic and the nonpneumatic not merely as between two worlds—the heavenly and the earthly—but also as between two ages (1 Cor. 15:46). The beginning of the pneumatic is the end of the present aeon. If the πνεῦμα has been at work, that proves that upon us τὰ τέλη τῶν αἰώνων κατήντηκεν. The parallel to this conclusion would be Paul's inferring τὸ πλήρωμα τοῦ χρόνου, in which Christ should appear (Gal. 4:4), from the actual presence of Christ in the world. But even the latter argument has the pneumatic experience of Christ as its presupposition.

So we will have to regard Weizsäcker's judgment as entirely correct: "Paul foots squarely on the soil of ancient popular faith when he sees evidences for [the presence of the kingdom of God], such as in Gal. 3:2ff., in the reception of the divine Spirit and all his activities."[24]

Thus we see first of all that Paul agrees to the greatest extent with the popular views.[25] But in 1 Cor. 12–14 we see the same man expressing a judgment and an evaluation of gifts which we may not assume for early apostolic circles and which until then—as is clear from the Epistle—was strange to the Corinthian church. Above all, Paul disparages glossolalia, which cannot be explained by what was said earlier of the composition of the primitive Christian community. Rather, what was stated above would more easily explain the behavior of the Corinthian church. For if that church conceived the Spirit as author wherever it sensed a mysterious, supernatural act of power, then it is entirely conceivable that glossolalia should appear to be the most significant, and for all Christians the most desirable, gift of the Spirit, with the result that glossolalia thoroughly dominated in the gatherings of the community. And we just as easily understand that individuals, prophets, and glossolalics alike claimed they could not

24. Weizsäcker, *Zeitalter,* p. 126.
25. Thus also the recognition and evaluation of gifts of the Spirit belong to the "neutral basis of the Pauline teaching" (Albrecht Ritschl, *Die Altkatholische Kirche* [Bonn, 1857], pp. 52ff.).

keep silent when the power of the Spirit "transported them and made them tremble" (En. 68:2). It is clear, of course, that it was not merely this by which the Corinthians incurred the apostle's displeasure. They had also indulged in the most disagreeable disputes regarding the value of the various gifts, disputes which often enough could assume a personal tone, so that the apostle had to force them to see that there are and must be different charismata in the community. It is also clear that such wild confusion prevailed in the gatherings that Paul had to emphasize the need for proper order. But even these events, these real excesses bitterly censured by Paul—and rightly so—still cohere in the popular view of the Spirit. If there were diverse gifts that had no unifying link except that they were generated in Christians by the same power, what was more natural than that they be compared and the attempt be made to establish the most valuable? Even the disorder in the worship assemblies is easy to understand, given the prevailing view of the Spirit and the agitation constantly nourished by it. These events are, therefore, not excesses of a singular nature. The deeper reason for these excesses was that the community lacked consciousness of the purpose, and therefore a proper criterion for evaluating the charismata. Paul stands here in a principle opposition to his community, and in this light he treated the entire question. For this reason he first developed his view of the charismata as such, in order to gain a base from which to correct the excesses at Corinth. Our description must proceed in the opposite direction, for to Paul's mind the practical question was primary and the theory throwing light on it was secondary.

For Paul, quite apart from his position with respect to the charismata, it was plain that such conditions as those which prevailed at Corinth are improper in a Christian community because the purpose of the community's coming together is the mutual edification of all its members. The community should come together εἰς τὸ κρεῖσσον (1 Cor. 11:17). Πάντα πρὸς οἰκοδομήν is the principle from which Paul proceeds. Where this chief purpose is not achieved, grave errors exist. For that reason, whatever does not serve the community does not belong in the gathering. Because of this, Paul almost totally excludes glossolalia. Only where there is interpretation that can edify the community may speaking in tongues occur, and even then to a most limited extent. To forbid glossolalia outright in the community gathering obviously was not feasible, given the circumstances then existing at Corinth. At the same time, Paul orders glossolalics as well as prophets to speak in sequence. Here too his motive is the disagreeable impression of the disorder that renders edification all but totally impossible. So all these commands follow not from Paul's concept of the charismata but from his view of the nature of Christian worship. The assumption underlying these regulations is that the bearers of the charismata are in a position to comply and to restrain the use of their gifts whenever they choose. He expressly stated this to prophets whose objection that they could not comply he must have anticipated. His thesis, πνεύματα προφητῶν προφήταις ὑποτάσσεται (1 Cor. 14:32), is thus a postulate that represents the needed basis for his commands. It is interesting to note how he establishes it: "For God is not a God of confusion but of peace" (v. 33). This is not an argument taken from the nature of prophecy, which adduces an experience gained by observing the usual behavior of prophets. We may question whether in every respect Paul's statement really amounted to this. Rather, this argument represents a certain conviction for every Christian, quite apart from prophecy and the charismata. The God who gives the charismata, who thus speaks in the prophets, does not intend disorder but rather desires quiet and order and thereby the edification of the church. God must therefore appoint the charismata in such a fashion that they are able to serve the divinely intended purpose. In this we perceive the principal difference between the Pauline view and the popular view. For the Christian community, the charismata are miracles to be wondered at, and the most valuable charisma is that in which the miraculous most clearly appears. There is no thought at all of its purpose. But for Paul the charismata have a divine intent, the οἰκοδομή of the community, and by that rule the worth of the individual gifts is determined.

Paul agrees with the Corinthian community that individual charismata have different value (12:31), but he maintains that the better a gift serves a community the more valuable that gift is. This shows why Paul declares glossolalia to be inferior—which is clear from the position this gift assumes in his enumerations in 1 Cor. 12:8ff.,28ff. (in Rom. 12:6ff. it is completely absent). But we must note especially that for Paul the idea of an activity of the Spirit is not altered by consideration of its purpose. He usually fixed the pneumatic origin of an appearance by its symptoms, just as his community did. This is clear from the fact that he thoroughly acknowledges as pneumatic an uninterpreted speaking in tongues, though he maintains it has no value for the community. The principle that "the gifts of the Spirit serve the mutual edification of the community" is thus not a judgment gleaned from experience but rather a requirement placed on pneumatics. To apply a modern device, it is not an analytical judgment but a synthetic one. Accordingly, the usual view, which is also represented by Wendt,[26] is untenable: "For Paul, that which best corresponds to the activities of the prophetic רוח in the Old Testament is a series of appearances of the Spirit of God which have as their common characteristic that they serve the community as such, that is, that they aim at the preservation, development, and expansion of the community." For Paul as well, this definition is false. The sole mark of the gifts of the Spirit is the appearing of a supernatural power in the Christian. If Wendt's definition were correct, then Paul would have had to regard uninterpreted glossolalia as nonpneumatic. To recognize this fact seems to us of decisive importance toward an understanding of the gifts of the Spirit in the New Testament age as a whole.[27] Incidentally, Paul assumes that even uninterpreted speaking in tongues edifies—naturally, the glossolalic himself. But this valuable activity was certainly not one of the symptoms by which bystanders fixed the actual presence of this working of the Spirit, since to ascertain the οἰκοδομή of another is something that naturally eludes judgment and, further, could only take place some time after the lapse of glossolalia.

In 1 Cor. 12:4–31 Paul more closely detailed and gave foundation to the rule Πάντα πϱὸς οἰκοδομήν. In these statements he is guided more

26. Wendt, *Begriffe*, p. 148. This view is also represented by Gloël, *Der heilige Geist*, p. 344: "According to Paul's fundamental view regarding the significance of the charismata, glossolalia could not have been viewed as a gift worked by the Spirit if some sort of διακονία for the community's sake had not been linked to it."

27. Hence the opinion that "a phenomenon is from the Spirit" rests on a direct impression of its enigmatic power, not on intelligent reflection regarding its use. Only this definition makes clear how the appearances of the Spirit could be the effluence and constant nourishment of primitive Christian enthusiasm.

and more by a broader point of view. He speaks not merely of charismata that may appear in the assemblies of a Christian community but also of the Christian community's gifts as such (the former in 1 Cor. 12:8–11, and the latter quite clearly in 28ff.). Verse 7, ἑκάστῳ δίδοται ἡ φανέρωσις τοῦ πνεύματος πρὸς τὸ συμφέρον, yields his main principle. Paul thus designates διακονία the correlative of χάρισμα, ἐνέργημα, or φανέρωσις τοῦ πνεύματος. The gift that God gives to the Christian should not be used for a mere display of supernatural power—it includes an obligation. The exercise of gifts of the Spirit is an action with ethical significance. Paul next graphically described this thought in the glorious figure (outlined in vv. 12ff.) of the Christian community as the body of Christ, members of which all Christians have become through the gift of the Spirit in baptism, and despite the variety of their service, for the good of the body (see also Rom. 12:4–8). If one of the practical lessons of this picture is that all Christians, despite their various charismata, belong to the body of Christ, that all are given the same Spirit to drink (see also 12:4ff.), then it is assumed here that the Corinthians were inclined to recognize only certain gifts as pneumatic. This supports our opinion that among the Corinthians, as well as in the first Christian communities generally, many regarded glossolalia as the sole utterance of the Spirit.

Another observation makes it clear that for Paul the gifts of the Spirit have ethical significance. According to the popular view, they most often erupt with the necessity of a natural event. Even Paul views his apostleship as under constraint: For if I preach the gospel, that gives me no ground for boasting; ἀνάγκη γάρ μοι ἐπίκειται. But it is an ethical necessity, the necessity of fulfilling an obligation, a feeling of responsibility—οὐαὶ γὰρ μοί ἐστιν, ἐάν μὴ εὐαγγελίζωμαι (1 Cor. 9:16)— for, to whom much is given, much will also be required.

What is also characteristic of Paul is the way in which he alters the Jewish impression of the nearness of the divine. It is Jewish to regard this mighty power that may also do harm first of all with dread and horror.[28] For Paul a grateful joy precedes it (see 1 Cor. 1:4; Phil. 1:3, etc.). And though the Christian who perceives in himself the Spirit's

28. See pp. 39–40.

sway experiences "fear and terror," it is not the dread of a supernatural power but rather the anxiety of allowing such a magnificent gift to be unused (see 1 Cor. 9:16; Phil. 2:12; 1 Thess. 4:8; see Eph. 4:30; Heb. 10:29).

Thus we also see that Paul prizes more highly than all the charismata an exercise of the Christian life not regarded as pneumatic by his age, that, in addition, he regards the most glorious gifts of the Spirit as nothing when love is lacking. It is, after all, love that gives them their worth. The charismata are the passing forms of that activity; their eternal content is love. That lofty hymn to love in 1 Corinthians 13, the most exalted passage we possess from the apostle's pen, clearly shows the towering height to which he was raised above his time: On the one hand, this community, embroiled in petty disputes over the value of individual gifts and the importance of single, ecstatic persons, this age, stock-still in reverent awe before individual, extraordinary phenomena in which it believed it felt the divine; and on the other hand the apostle, himself a pneumatic, who nevertheless sets all these glorified supernatural experiences, in which he too believes, back of what is simple, natural, and everyone's affair, who regards all expressions of the Spirit as nothing in face of the one, high, and glorious thing—love.

To what degree are these statements of Paul original? Obviously, many members of the primitive church used their pneumatic talent for the good of the community. We may not attribute to them the annoyances of the Corinthian church. And the eternal prototype of love which sets all it has in the service of the brethren is not Paul but Someone higher. The requirement of the apostle, πάντα πρὸς οἰκοδομήν, is finally nothing but the consequence of the parable in Matt. 25:14–30; of course, we will hardly contend that Paul had that parable in mind. Thus, what he requires is still to be judged as something new. Yet, even in this respect Paul is certainly not the initiator of a new life. But he has put into words what was alive in him and in others, and what he devised is not an unfruitful theory. Till that moment the door to enthusiasm and disorder was ajar; the gifts of the Spirit might lead to the ruin of all Christian community relationships. It was Paul's service, alongside his lofty and inspiring view of the "community as the body of Christ," to have furnished a solid criterion by which gifts of the Spirit could be judged and evaluated from that moment on.

GIFTS OF THE SPIRIT PECULIAR TO
PAUL'S THEOLOGY

Thus far we have seen that Paul first of all distances himself from the view prevalent in the churches not by his recognition of the individual gifts of the Spirit as such but by his ethical evaluation of these gifts. If this raises him to a dizzying height above common opinion, this is even more the case at still another point. Paul sees the activities of the Spirit in an abundance of Christian functions, which Judaism and the earliest Christian communities did not regard as the activities of a supernatural power. They are consciousness of the love of God (Rom. 5:5), joy over the salvation received (1 Thess. 1:6; Rom. 14:17), and hope in the consummation (Rom. 15:13; Gal. 5:5)—they are love, joy, peace, patience, kindness, goodness, faithfulness, gentleness, self-control (Gal. 5:22–23). In a word, all Christian existence should be guided by the norm of the Spirit (κατὰ πνεῦμα περιπατεῖν: Rom. 8:4; φρονεῖν τὰ τοῦ πνεύματος: Rom. 8:5) because it can be led by the power of the Spirit (πνεύματι περιπατεῖν, στοιχεῖν: Gal. 5:16,25). The Christian as such is πνευματικός (1 Cor. 2:15; 3:1).[29]

What is surprising here is that the very basic fact of Christian existence, that by which a person becomes a Christian, is nowhere expressly noted as a work of the Spirit. This statement cannot be countered with 2 Cor. 4:13 any more than with, for example, 1 Cor. 12:9 (πίστις as χάρισμα), which refers to a special, "pneumatic" faith. This circumstance is all the more surprising since Paul views conversion and faith with complete assurance as the work of God in man (see Phil. 3:12; 1:29; Rom. 12:3; 1 Cor. 12:3; 2 Cor. 3:3; and esp. 1 Thess. 1:6). Nevertheless for Paul and for the earliest Christian communities, faith is the presupposition for the reception of the Spirit (this is particularly clear in Gal. 3:14),[30] and for him as well the gift of the Spirit is given in baptism (1 Cor. 12:13; see 6:11; a different view is in Gal. 3:2). The latter must have been a daily experience in the first

29. Our intention in this treatise is not to give a description of individual activities of the Spirit, and thus here a description of the Christian life as Paul idealized it. That is no more our intention than when we characterized individual charismata in Chapter 1. We merely note what types of human functions are taken to be pneumatic and inquire as to why just these are regarded as activities of the Spirit; see pp. 9–10.

30. See Gloël, *Der heilige Geist,* pp. 97ff., 101.

Christian communities. The miraculous powers of the Spirit began to show themselves in baptism. This, then, explains the Pauline principle. It simply follows the ideas of the primitive Christian community and commences pneumatic existence at the point where the community conceives of the gifts as present in Christians.

Paul's Utterances in Light of His Own Experience

How did these sayings of the apostle arise regarding the Christian's walk in the Spirit? We have the answer when we inquire into their meaning. In particular, it was Wendt's service to have laid stress on the fact that for Paul the Spirit is a power.[31] Wendt correctly indicates "that in many passages, the concepts πνεῦμα and δύναμις are directly connected with each other," and "that in a few other passages the word δύναμις can actually appear alone and in place of πνεῦμα."[32] When Wendt calls this idea of the πνεῦμα an Old Testament idea, then, according to what was stated above, we may add that it is also the Jewish and early apostolic view—an observation which seems far more important to us since it also gives the explanation as to the source of Paul's identification of πνεῦμα and δύναμις. If we ask how Paul's teaching concerning the Christian life as an activity of the πνεῦμα is to be understood, then we should recall his experience of "the power and depth of his spiritual inspiration," by which "he felt his entire life constantly filled and driven by the power of the Spirit of Christ."[33] We would thus call his πνεῦμα-doctrine an expression of

---

31. Wendt, *Begriffe,* pp. 145–46; see also Weiss, *Lehrbuch,* p. 328, n. 4. Of course, this accurate perception does not prevent Wendt from conceiving the Spirit as a name "for the entire range of supernatural acts of power which manifest themselves in various ways" (*Begriffe,* p. 140). The same confusion of a principle of acts of power and their complex still appears in Wendt, *Begriffe,* on pp. 32 and 35 (the Spirit is a "mood"), and often in Ernst Issel, *Der Begriffe der Heiligkeit im Neuen Testament* (Leiden, 1887), pp. 55, 56 (the Spirit is the "certainty of salvation"). This error of Wendt and Issel is rightly censured by Gloël, *Der heilige Geist,* pp. 373–74. The reason for such confusion is not simply a logical error, for then it would scarcely deserve mention. The ultimate reason is simply that modern theology is striving to recognize the Spirit as an objectively present entity. Thus the Spirit alive in the Christian community is often referred to merely as a "spirit" that may also be present in another fellowship. Accordingly, the Spirit is thought of merely as "a specific form of human self-consciousness," a totality of purposes, motives, and powers. Now, whatever opinion dogmatics may hand down in the matter, it is in any event the duty of the exegete to protest against all modernizations of New Testament views; see Gloël, *Der heilige Geist,* pp. 374–75.

32. Evidences in Wendt, *Begriffe,* p. 146.

33. Otto Pfleiderer, *Urchristentum* (Berlin, 1887), p. 257.

that glorious feeling of power by which he could exclaim, πάντα ἰσχύω ἐν τῷ ἐνδυναμοῦντί με! But this answer is still not sufficient. Spirit is not power absolutely. Spirit is the divine, supernatural power, and when Paul asserts that the entire conduct of the Christian is an activity of God's Spirit, he is saying that there is a power manifest in the Christian life which is divine, that is, absolutely supernatural, and which can never be explained by human powers or by this aeon.

The Christian possesses a force more mighty than the natural man. What the latter could not do, the former is able to do. The natural man languished under the reign of sin; the Christian has become free from it. It was impossible for the Jew to keep the Law; Christian love is the fulfillment of the Law. The demons with dark impulse led the heathen astray to dumb idols; the Christian is able to cry, "Jesus is Lord." Thus a person cannot by himself create that mode of life which seizes the Christian; he cannot attain to the power over which the Christian disposes. This power is absolutely suprahuman. Therefore, in whomever this power dwells, he "receives" it (1 Cor. 2:12; Gal. 3:2,14; 2 Cor. 11:4; Rom. 8:15). It is "given" to him (2 Cor. 1:22; 5:5; Rom. 5:5; 1 Thess. 4:8), "supplied" (Gal. 3:5), and "sent" (Gal. 4:6). This power is "experienced" (endured: παθεῖν), as are its activities (Gal. 3:4). Its activities are gifts of grace. But even those in whom this power continually resides always remain recipients, passive over against it. The Christian is "led" by it (Gal. 5:18; Rom. 8:14). He is under its "law" (Rom. 8:2). It is his master whose commands he obeys (δουλεύειν: Rom. 7:6). Now, the apostle does not conceive this power energizing the Christian as something alien, something external to him and summoning him. Rather its effect is precisely that of taking hold of the person himself and altering his entire way of life.[34] Paul gave most pointed expression to the idea that the Christian is under a lordship originally foreign to his "I" by conceiving the two opposing principles of human activity as working on him from without: ταῦτα ἀλλήλοις ἀντίκειται, ἵνα μὴ ὃ ἐὰν θέλητε ταῦτα ποιῆτε (Gal. 5:17). Whoever is subject to either principle no longer does what he himself desires; he must act as he is commanded, whether he will or not. This may not be the apostle's usual manner of speaking, but it is still clear what he intends to say: The

---

34. See the beautiful description in ibid., pp. 263ff.

power that rules the Christian is absolutely superhuman; it is originally foreign to the ego and thus not at all a universal human capacity, and it rules over him so absolutely that it does not allow him to carry out his own will at all.

The Christian life therefore rests upon a power that would be an impenetrable mystery if it were explained in terms of human capabilities. But this force is even stronger. It exceeds by far everything that usually rules on earth. It is stronger than sin; it conquers sin. It is stronger than the Law; it effects what the Law was not able to do. And, stronger than the demons, it wrests men from their dominion. Thus, this power is actually transcendent. It cannot be explained in terms of the world at hand. If its activities should have their origin in the world, they would remain an insoluble puzzle, an inexplicable mystery. Consequently, the ordinary person is not in a position to appreciate and understand the Christian life. "It is utterly impossible for the natural man to probe the inner nature of the person filled with the Spirit and to do it justice. For him, the pneumatic is an unfathomable enigma. As the blind man responds to the beauty of color, the deaf man to the harmony of tones, the man without imagination to the power of poetic art,"[35] so the ordinary person responds to these phenomena. Who can be that mysterious power beneath such mighty activities?

To these questions the apostle answers that it is the miraculously working Spirit of God which performed this miracle, for it is clear that it is the Spirit of God. But the Spirit comes only on those who have come to faith in God through Christ, and in them he works God's will. The Christian life is a disposition of the $\pi\nu\epsilon\hat{\nu}\mu\alpha$, which for Paul means that the Christian life is absolutely inconceivable in earthly terms; it is a miracle of God.[36]

The teaching concerning the $\pi\nu\epsilon\hat{\nu}\mu\alpha$ gives this impression. Paul gives the same impression when he states that the Christian is an ἔργον τοῦ θεοῦ (Rom. 14:20) and a καινὴ κτίσις (Gal. 6:15; 2 Cor. 5:17) and the

---

35. From Gloël, *Der heilige Geist,* p. 233.

36. In this opinion we concur completely with the principle recently enunciated by Harnack, *Lehrbuch,* 1:47, n. 1: "In the Spirit of adoption there was experience of a totally new gift from God transforming existence—*a miracle of God. For this very reason, the spirit of ecstasy as well as of miracles seemed to be identical with the Spirit.*"

community an οἰκοδομὴ τοῦ ϑεοῦ (1 Cor. 3:9). Christian existence is something totally new, something absolutely inexplicable in terms of the world at hand as was the old κτίσις. In midst of the old world the Christian is newly created by God. The one begotten of the Spirit is not τοῦ αἰῶνος τούτου but a child of the Jerusalem above (Gal. 4:26). There is the same impression underlying Paul's reference to himself as the father of his converts, to conversion as a begetting in the Lord, or to the converted as his children in Christ.

This also makes clear how Paul conceives conversion. To become a Christian means to make a complete break with all that was prior, "to die to the world," to become a new person. The Christian existence is not a product organically developing from earlier existence. Between the Christian's life now and his Jewish or heathen past there is no psychological means of building a span or of explaining the later from the earlier. Christian existence comes into being through a break, through the intervention of something supernatural, something new, that is, through the intervention of the Spirit of God.

It is easy to perceive the origin of Paul's impression of the Christian life. He received it for the first time when he himself was "seized" by a higher hand (Phil. 3:12), when there dawned on him a recognition as new and unexpected as the appearing of light in darkness, to be conceived only as an act of God, just as the first creation when God said, "Let light shine out of darkness" (2 Cor. 4:6). Thus the root of the apostle's teaching concerning the πνεῦμα lies in his experience. And as often as he later saw that the foolishness of God was wiser than men and the weakness of God stronger than men, that the power of God is mighty precisely in its weakness, he continually recognized that man may do nothing by his own natural powers, may do all things in him who strengthens him.

Let us review. The entire life of the Christian is an activity of the πνεῦμα. This means that the entire life of the Christian reveals a powerful, transcendent, divine power. It is thus the same manner of inferring the Spirit as was used in the Christian community prior to Paul. For Paul too an activity of the Spirit is that in which an inexplicable power, the mysterious and mighty, is manifest. Every activity of the Spirit is a miracle. Thus Paul's view of the πνεῦμα is exactly the same as that of the primitive Christian community. Paul, just as others in his time, thinks in thoroughly supernaturalistic fashion. And yet what a change in this Pauline idea! The same judgment that the popular view gives of a few definitely extraordinary appearances, Paul gives of the entire Christian life. Prophecy, glossolalia, and the like may appear mysterious to the Christian community, but Paul knows of something else that is just as great a divine enigma to him. The community thus regards as pneumatic what is extraordinary in Christian existence, but Paul what is usual; the community what is individual and unique, but Paul what is common to all; the community what abruptly appears, but Paul what is constant; the community what is isolated in Christian existence, but Paul the Christian life as such. And this yielded a totally different, infinitely higher evaluation of Christian conduct. Of course for Paul too the conviction that "an appearance is an activity of the Spirit" is not a judgment as to value but rather a judgment as to its source. But it is clear that a judgment which perceives the divine origin of an appearance results in its especially high evaluation. Thus, the value that the primitive Christian community gives to these miracles Paul gives to Christian existence itself. It is no longer the single or sporadic that constitutes the divine in man. Rather, the Christian is the pneumatic. We do not hesitate to assert that this idea is one of Paul's most ingenious and truly pneumatic conceptions. There is here a most glorious blending of the most vivid view of the Spirit with the most valuable content of this form. "This established Christianity in its independence from Judaism as a new historical principle and at the same time bridged the gap between the ecstatic, enthusiastic phenomena of the primitive community and a steady, historical development of the community."[37] The gifts of the Spirit in the apostolic age have vanished, though in isolated Christian circles something similar may perhaps be observed to this day. But we can also do without these miraculous gifts. For even now we daily perceive other activities of the Spirit in our life. Even for us, the Christian is a miracle of God.[38]

37. Pfleiderer, *Paulinismus,* p. 200.
38. For the most part we agree with Pfleiderer (ibid., pp. 199ff.; *Urchristentum,* pp. 255–57) in this comparison and evaluation of the popular and Pauline view. We part company with him in the interpretation of the proper sense and origin of the Pauline teaching.

Thus we see that the further development of primitive Christian views which we established as occurring in Paul conforms throughout to the experience of his life and is fully explained by it.

Other Explanations

Wendt offers an opinion that is totally different from our own.[39] He compares the Pauline doctrine with a few Old Testament passages in which he finds the same thought expressed and writes that "there is thus no sufficient reason for seeing in Paul's teaching of the religious-ethical value [that must mean, of the religious-ethical *activity*] of the divine πνεῦμα a particularly new transformation of the traditional doctrine."[40]

First of all, let us more carefully consider the passages compared by Wendt. He cites Zech. 12:10, Ezek. 11:19–20, 36:26–27, Isa. 4:4, 28:6, 32:15ff., and 42:1. Ezek. 11:19–20 and 36:26, which refer to a רוח חדשה which God will some day give the Jews, do not apply here at all since this "new spirit" has nothing whatever to do with the רוח י'. In these two passages "spirit" denotes the spirit of man, in this instance, his character. This is certainly clear from the parallelism with לב; from the distinction in Ezek. 36:26–27 between רוח חדשה and רוחי (=רוח י'), and further from Ezek. 18:31, in which the Jews are summoned to obtain (עשה) a לב חדש ורוח חדשה, which could not possibly be said of the divine Spirit.[41] Further, how the רוח משפט in Isa. 4:4 is to be understood must remain problematic.[42] Still further, Isa. 42:1 does not refer to the religious-moral behavior of the Servant of Yahweh, for which the רוח should equip him. Rather, the Servant of Yahweh is equipped with the Spirit in order to carry out his teaching office among the people. For us everything hangs on distinguishing clearly between activities of the Spirit which have

39. Wendt, *Begriffe*, pp. 152–53.

40. Ibid., p. 153.

41. These observations also hold true against Gloël (*Der heilige Geist,* p. 238), who follows Wendt here. Further, on p. 30 Wendt himself cites Ezek. 11:19 to prove that רוח and לב "have a closely related meaning," and clearly distinguishes this meaning of רוח from the רוח of God (p. 32). Then on p. 153 Wendt appears to have forgotten his accurate interpretation of Ezek. 11:19. Indeed, Gloël even exceeds Wendt's error by confusing the רוח חדשה in Ezek. 18:30–31, which the sinful Israelites should obtain, with the רוח י'.

42. See p. 15.

ethical-religious value and those which actually occur within the sphere of the ethical-religious.[43] On the other hand, in Ezek. 36:27,[44] Isa. 28:6, and 32:15ff.—to which Zech. 12:10 may be compared—the Spirit appears as a principle of the religious and moral. In addition, there are passages not cited by Wendt—Isa. 11:2, Ps. 51:13, and 143:10—of which the last two have by far the greatest significance for our question, since they show the teaching concerning the Spirit in its relation to the life of the individual believer.

First, what is the sense of those prophetic passages that promise the Spirit will create justice and righteousness among the people and its rulers in the end time? They signify that the prophets despair of moving the people to do Yahweh's will by their preaching and that for this reason they are convinced God himself must intervene to create the ideal situation he requires. Thus the ideal kingdom in which piety and righteousness dwell cannot be a product of the people's natural development. It can only come about by an act of God, by a miracle, by the outpouring of the Spirit of God. "At the same time, the impression that these hindrances made was so great that the prophets imagined the goal could be reached only on condition of a breach in history."[45] These prophetic ideas are, of course, parallel to the views of Paul. Both Paul and the prophets infer from their experience of man's or the people's incapacity for righteousness that the conduct which is truly pleasing to God does not result from human initiative but is rather the work of the divine Spirit. Nevertheless, the difference between the two sequences of ideas is also not to be ignored. In their utterances the prophets express an unshakable conviction that the ideal must still be realized despite all which for a time opposes it, and for them it is only the righteousness of the end time which is pneumatic. But for Paul each Christian act is a divine mystery and thus pneumatic, and what he calls a work of the Spirit is something which gives him and his fellow Christians joy in the present. Thus the prophets hope, but Paul possesses. The prophetic passages,

---

43. See pp. 22–23.
44. Ezek. 39:29 is also to be interpreted according to Ezek. 36:27.
45. Albrecht Ritschl, *Rechtfertigung und Versöhnung,* 2d ed. (Bonn, 1882), 2:28.

especially those in Isaiah, are of course very close to Paul, but they are also characteristically different from him. Paul stands incomparably higher.[46]

Much closer to the Pauline view is the conviction expressed in Ps. 51:13 and 143:10. Here the poets, overwhelmed by the feeling that a man conceived and born in sin (Ps. 51:7) cannot stand in God's judgment (Ps. 143:2), pray for aid from God's holy and good Spirit. The one who is weak prays for power from above. This is really parallel to the Pauline ideas except that the apostle's rock-firm conviction that he has the Spirit deviates significantly from this sighing for the granting of the Spirit. In any case, it is most remarkable that the idea expressed in those verses no longer appears in psalms that still contain so many prayers similar to Psalms 51 and 143—clear proof of our thesis that for Judaism the piety of the ordinary man on the whole appeared to have nothing in common with the רוח.

With these observations in mind we are able to test Wendt's thesis that Paul appropriated his doctrine of the moral and religious activities of the πνεῦμα from the Old Testament. To be sure, the Old Testament passages that he cites contain similar ideas. At first, then, we have nothing against Wendt's statement. But it must be noted that Paul neither cites nor alludes to those prophetic utterances in which the descent of the Spirit is predicted. The same is true of Ps. 51:13 and 143:10. Paul never once mentions that the outpouring of the Spirit was promised by the prophets. We would expect him to make frequent mention of this point if these prophetic oracles had such great significance for him that they became the basis of a doctrine so important to him.[47] But the real objection to Wendt's opinion is that it is

46. Zech. 12:10 does not express the dogmatic principle that the Spirit "works supplication and prayer." Rather, in a quite concrete situation the prophet hopes the Spirit may do so for his obdurate contemporaries. The passage in Zechariah is similar to such passages as Rom. 8:15,26 and Gal. 4:6 (see Wendt, *Begriffe*, pp. 152–53; Gloël, *Der heilige Geist*, pp. 203–4), which refer to ecstatic prayers only insofar as Zechariah and Paul assume that the Spirit *can* effect the mood of prayer. Further, it is highly questionable whether the translation "supplication and prayer" (not "compassion and mercy") is accurate.

47. We reckon the passage in Eph. 1:13 to the Deutero-Pauline literature. Naturally, whether one assents to this judgment or not, the point at issue is not changed at all.

grounded on a false conception of the development of Paul's thought. The theology of the great apostle is the expression of his experience, not of his reading. The Old Testament might suggest to him the one or other idea, but it is not the basis for his teaching. Should Paul really have created this vivid view of the πνεῦμα, in which he unveils for us the profoundest depths of his conviction, of his experience, on the basis of his reading?

We must judge in quite different fashion the statement of Pfleiderer to the effect that Paul's teaching on the subject rests partly on his experience, partly on Hellenistic views.[48] Here the issue is no longer the influence of Paul's reading (though in only a very limited sense can we concede Pfleiderer's statement regarding the great influence of The Wisdom of Solomon on Paul) but that of his education and everyday communication. Since we cannot from the outset evaluate the significance of these factors for Paul, such an assumption of Hellenistic influence is not to be rejected *a limine* but rather to be tested quite impartially. At issue in this instance is the relation between Paul's teaching concerning the πνεῦμα and that of The Wisdom of Solomon, which shows, according to Pfleiderer's version, "that from the height the divine wisdom or the holy spirit makes the souls in which it finds its dwelling friends of God and prophets, equips them with all knowledge and all virtue, and even makes them share in eternal life (see The Wisdom of Solomon, chaps. 7, 8, 9)." The similarity between these sequences of ideas and those in Paul is rather striking, but it lies essentially in the form—the contents are very different.

Paul believes in the divine Spirit because he has experienced it. The apocryphal book speculates concerning wisdom and combines it with the totally faded concept of the Spirit of God as taken from the tradition. For Paul the Spirit is the power of God which transforms him in his innermost being; for The Wisdom of Solomon wisdom is the teacher who instructs regarding God's paths (7:22; 8:9; 9:10–11; 10:10). A man learns wisdom, but the Spirit seizes him. Thus, all the statements of The Wisdom of Solomon and of Paul, as similar as they may appear, have an entirely different meaning.

48. Pfleiderer, *Urchristentum,* p. 257.

Wisdom equips one with all the virtues because they arise out of her instruction (6:17ff.; 8:7). The Spirit also dispenses all virtues, but he does so because he effects them as a power of God in man.

Wisdom preserves the righteous man blameless through her instruction (10:5,13); in the former sinful man, the Spirit creates a struggle against the flesh.

Wisdom makes friends of God, "for God loves nothing so much as the man who lives with wisdom" (7:28; see 4:10; 7:14; 9:12), but the Spirit is given to the one who receives the electing love of God in faith.

"Immortality" is the reward for a life led in wisdom, "for good labors bring forth good fruits" (3:15; see 1:15; 2:22; 3:5; 3:14; 5:15–16; 8:13,17; 10:17), but the Spirit is the power of a new, eternal life.

What is the reason for the difference?

Paul is the apostle of Jesus Christ who testifies to what he experienced. Contrariwise, the author of The Wisdom of Solomon is a philosopher of religion, not uninfluenced by Greek thought, whose speculation in essence rests on a moralistic foundation and is only slightly altered by a type of religious perception proceeding from earnest piety (e.g., 7:7; esp. 8:21: God gives wisdom; 9:9–18). It is thus a mode of instruction which is congenial, for example, with that of the apostolic fathers and which differs from them only by its speculative posture.

So then, the utterances of Paul and The Wisdom of Solomon are not at all related in kind. It is therefore highly unlikely that Paul borrowed from such a sequence of ideas. And the very point at which religious speculation on our subject begins to show itself in Paul[49]—I mean the idea of the Spirit as principle of a transcendent, hidden existence—does not appear in The Wisdom of Solomon. If it were true that we could find no explanation for Paul's doctrine of the Spirit, we might still assume that he took up the concept of wisdom as developed by Jewish-Hellenistic speculation and gave it such an altogether different stamp, with the result that he "fashioned from theosophic ideas religious realities of a concrete, easily perceptible content and agreeable force for motivation."[50] But since we can adequately

49. See pp. 110–111.
50. Pfleiderer, *Urchristentum*, p. 258.

explain his view of the Spirit from that of early Christianity, nothing compels us to this assumption.

Thus, over against Wendt and Pfleiderer,[51] we will have to maintain the essential originality of Paul's teaching. Our decision is that Paul found ready-made the concept of the πνεῦμα as a wonder-working power, but on the basis of his experience, by which the Christian himself appeared to be the greatest miracle, he described the Christian life as an activity of the πνεῦμα in a completely original way.

Paul's originality is confirmed throughout when we contrast his idea of the πνεῦμα with that of Judaism, to the extent that this idea can be recognized in "Palestinian-Jewish literature." There the prophecy is simply repeated that the righteousness of the end time and its king will be a work of the divine Spirit (see En. 49:3-4; 62:2; Ps. Sol. 17:42; 18:8; Bk. Jub. 1; Testament of Judah 24; Testament of Levi 18). Further, the Spirit is regarded as the power of the heavenly kingdom: "In the spirit of faith, and in the spirit of wisdom, and in the spirit of patience, and in the spirit of mercy, and in the spirit of judgment and of peace, and in the spirit of goodness," the angels praise the great deeds of the highest before his throne (En. 61:11). Thus, the opinion in Judaism is that the Spirit may also have moral and religious effects, indeed, that the highest piety and morality—as the angels now enjoy it and as one day those who share in the messianic splendor will enjoy it—is given by the Spirit. But one's own life of faith is not derived from the Spirit. The ordinary conduct of a man does not give the impression that it is of supernatural origin. Not even John the Baptist regards the "conversion" to which he calls men as pneumatic; he well knows he can do nothing more than baptize with water. But the One who is to come will baptize with the Spirit and with fire, that is, in the power of the Spirit he will purge the sins of Israel and thus bring true cleansing.

One might, perhaps, judge Paul's originality differently when he compares The Testaments of the Twelve Patriarchs and, of course, those portions that according to Schnapp's analysis[52] do not in any case belong to the Christian redactor. Here an idea is expressed which

---

51. And we cannot sanction Pfleiderer's previous attempt to derive the Pauline teaching concerning the πνεῦμα from the doctrine of Christ (*Paulinismus,* pp. 202ff.). See p. 115.

52. See Friedrich Schnapp, *Die Testamente der 12 Patriarchen* (Halle, 1884).

is similar to that in The Shepherd of Hermas. The author, given to fantasy, sees good and evil spirits everywhere at work. Just as Judaism as a whole conceives of heaven and earth as filled with spirits that exercise the most varied functions and are not clearly differentiated from the angels, so the author of The Testaments derives every human deed, every resolve, every thought from spirits. He even conceives of the seven senses as spirits (see Testament of Reuben 2). Though more interested by far in the evil spirits, to which his fantasy is obviously more attached, in a few passages (Testament of Simeon 4; Testament of Benjamin 4:8; see Testament of Judah 20) he still speaks of the "spirit of truth" who works good, who proceeds from God and who is also called the "spirit of God" (Testament of Simeon 4, after Gen. 41:38). Underlying this entire imaginative idea is nothing but the observation that the passions of men, and likewise their conscience (because that is the "spirit of truth"), have a certain power over whoever heeds them. We will probably not judge too harshly when we trace such ideas to the author's imagination rather than to his religious life and thus deny them any religious worth. Paul's teaching concerning the πνεῦμα, reflecting his religious experiences, is thus totally independent even of such certainly widespread Jewish opinions.

Gloël attacks Paul's originality from another side when he states that we may be sure "that the fundamental witness of the Lord and of his first apostles did not lack a sense for the morally determinant activity of the Spirit."[53]

By this statement, of course, Gloël does not intend to deny the "inner independence of the Pauline views," the source of which he also regards as the apostle's experience.[54] But Paul was not at all the only one in his day to make such utterance; the Lord himself and the witness of the apostles had gone before him.

As proof of his contention, Gloël cites John, 1 Peter, and Acts. We have already referred to Acts and have seen that it in no way presents the Christian life as such as an activity of the Spirit.[55] We will therefore not return to this source here. And Gloël's reference to the

---

53. Gloël, Der heilige Geist, pp. 238ff.
54. Ibid., p. 241.
55. See pp. 17–18.

ἁγιασμὸς πνεύματος in 1 Pet. 1:2—incidentally, the only passage in
1 Peter which can come up for consideration here—scarcely requires
comment since it is not clear what sort of activity the author of the
Epistle has in mind. But if—as Gloël is inclined to assume and we for
our part think likely—the πνεῦμα should be thought of as the power
that establishes the Christian life, there would still be the question as
to whether or not 1 Peter is dependent on Paul at this juncture. The
same applies to the Gospel of John. It is true that John 3:5,6 and so on
offer analogies to the Pauline ideas. But it is quite remarkable that in
the preaching of the Lord according to the synoptic Gospels, such
utterances are totally lacking (see the variant readings on Luke 9:55;
on Luke 11:13, see Matt. 7:11). This fact, which Gloël seems to
ignore, raises the question whether or not this teaching concerning the
πνεῦμα should be assigned to the author of the Gospel of John and not
the historical Jesus. Now, when we examine the critical passage in
John 3 more closely and ask whether the attitude of the Lord toward
Nicodemus described there conforms to the synoptic picture of Jesus,
then we must answer in the negative. The Jesus of the synoptic
Gospels never spoke as Christ is here reported to speak to Nicodemus.
The Jesus of the synoptic Gospels preaches in order to be understood,
but the other speaks so that the Jew cannot understand him at all. One
can only speak of the significance of the divine Spirit for new birth to
someone who has already had the same experiences. These are
statements which have their echo in the Christian's breast, which have
deep meaning for the advanced understanding of a Christian community but which must remain unintelligible to the ἰδιώτης. The
evangelist writes, but the Lord does not preach, in this fashion.

But even aside from this we are in great disagreement with Gloël. To
the question whether Pauline influence can be detected in the πνεῦμα-
doctrine of 1 Peter, analogous to Paul's teaching, or of the Gospel of
John, Gloël answers in the negative: "With regard to Old Testament
utterances having the same tendency, the tracing of the clues that we
have identified to Pauline influence is superfluous."[56] So it is his
opinion that a teaching concerning the πνεῦμα such as Paul's was not
at all something very original: "Even this did not lack points of
contact in the Old Testament."[57]

56. Gloël, *Der heilige Geist*, p. 240.
57. Ibid., p. 237.

104

Indeed, "to the essential portions of prophetic expectation there no doubt" belonged "the hope which found such unequivocal expression in Ezekiel 36."[58] Thus, despite his reference to Paul's experience, Gloël repeats Wendt's contention concerning Old Testament influence on this Pauline teaching. Unfortunately, he did not add how we are to understand why Paul in one instance reflects an independence in these utterances[59] and in the next still "attaches" to the Old Testament.[60] I regret that Gloël has not dealt with this question—which I take to be one of the most important in this area—in the same detail as with other, perhaps less essential questions. Does Gloël perhaps think that this doctrine of Paul was widespread in Judaism because it was contained in the Old Testament? That would be decidedly false.[61] Or does he think this doctrine originated in Paul's mind in such fashion that the apostle correctly read his experiences of a divine and mighty power which totally filled, hallowed, renewed, and liberated him only when he combined those experiences with the prophetic prediction, and thus saw in them the sway of the divine Spirit? Indeed, I would very much doubt the accuracy of such a construction. For the apostle, the Spirit is a view so clear and so familiar that he did not require Old Testament reminiscences in order to say to himself, "This power in me, which raises me above myself and has transformed and daily transforms me into a new creation, can only be the Spirit."[62] The reason for this lack of clarity in Gloël is that he never once asks why Paul called the πνεῦμα the power initiating all these experiences. This question, which we tried to answer above, the truly chief biblical-theological problem in the entire discussion, Gloël has not recognized, and for that reason he cannot evaluate Paul's great originality. But I fear that where this problem is not seen and correctly answered the apostle's teaching concerning the πνεῦμα, in the last analysis, remains unintelligible. For the apostle, his existence was an enigma to which

58. Ibid., p. 240.
59. Ibid., p. 241.
60. Ibid., p. 237.
61. See pp. 19–21.
62. Thus I contend that there is actually the fulfillment of an Old Testament prophecy here, and indeed, a fulfillment that occurred in precisely the sense originally intended. Totally independent of the prophets, Paul experienced and confessed what they had prophesied. But for Gloël it would still be only a fulfillment contrived by human ingenuity, as in 2 Kings 9:25–26.

his teaching regarding the πνεῦμα gave the solution; for us that teaching is an enigma to which the apostle's life and only his life can give the solution.

THE RELATION OF THREE TYPES OF INFLUENCE OF THE SPIRIT

We must not overlook the fact that for Paul the two major areas in which the divine spirit proves he is even now at work are originally of a very disparate nature.[63] First of all, according to Paul's view, the Christian life and the charismata have nothing more in common than that they are of supernatural origin. But the apostle does not sense this difference. " 'Spirit' and 'spirit' were still intertwined." This is not surprising, since even those special gifts are for Paul functions with ethical significance. And we ought not forget that even in the early apostolic view the limits of the supernatural and natural could not, by the very nature of the case, be always sharply drawn. For Paul, however, the miraculous gifts are only a special activity of the same Spirit who is also miraculously at work in all Christians and in every age. Paul draws no real limit between the two types of spiritual phenomena, as can be seen, for example, in Rom. 12:6ff., where the apostle moves from an enumeration of the Christian charismata to that of the Christian virtues. For him even the virtues, which just as the charismata are variously manifest in individuals, are "gifts of grace" (1 Cor. 7:7). The result is that when Paul speaks of the πνεῦμα, very often we cannot say which of these two types of activities he has in mind. For example, the wisdom of which Paul speaks in 1 Cor. 1:24 and 2:6ff. is a wisdom given to all Christians, but again it is also a special wisdom in which the apostle rejoices.[64]

Thus, when Paul speaks of the Spirit as the guarantor of the

---

63. See Harnack, *Lehrbuch,* 1:47, n. 1.

64. Gloël also emphasizes the "inner connection between the religious, ennobling activity of the Spirit and that which is active in the charismata," *Der heilige Geist,* pp. 355–56. On the same page he refers to the πίστις of 1 Cor. 13:2, which, among other things, still has "its deepest roots in saving faith." But when Gloël ventures the statement that "the equipping of the Christian with gifts of grace" occurs "entirely in relation to the ethical calling which the one walking in the Spirit receives in the community" (p. 357), such a view appropriate to the Reformation period can scarcely be proved from Paul. For Paul what is at issue is only that with a charisma one also receives a calling—not the reverse.

Christian hope, he often has in mind the Spirit as the principle of Christian conduct. This idea can be utilized in a twofold way. Either the inference is drawn from the joyous feeling of walking in the Spirit now, in the present, that eternal life will also be the gift of this same Spirit (thus Rom. 8:11,14–17; see Rom. 6:22; 2 Cor. 1:22; 5:5), or the idea is sharpened in the admonition that only he who walks in the Spirit will have life in the Spirit (Gal. 6:8; Rom. 8:12–13). Here therefore Christian conduct and eternal life are thought of as two separate activities of the Spirit, which, however, stand in organic connection with each other. The result of walking in the Spirit is eternal life, just as surely and naturally as fruit results from the seed. It is obvious, according to what was stated above, that such an evaluation of Christian conduct is specifically Pauline.[65] But in essence Paul would still remain within the context of the ancient Christian perspective when he regards the real blessing of the messianic kingdom, the ζωὴ αἰώνιος, as future (Rom. 2:7; 5:21; 6:22–23; Gal. 6:8; 2 Cor. 5:4; Phil. 4:3) and recognizes only certain activities of the Spirit as signs in the present of what is to come and which allow its glory to be surmised. But alongside this perspective, quite common even to Paul, there is also the other, by which the "life" has already become the possession of Christians now. We must examine in what sense Paul speaks of the already existent, spirit-worked "life" of Christians, especially in Rom. 8:10 and Gal. 5:25.

It is not appropriate to divide this concept into two halves with Wendt,[66] and to assert that the πνεῦμα τῆς ζωῆς is "either the power of supernatural life in the heavenly state of existence or the power of moral activity during one's earthly life,"[67] and thus to assign life to the person now living only in terms of moral energy. For when Paul speaks of "life," he sums up in this term all the blessings of the messianic kingdom. "Life" is also for him "the essence of the divine blessing and promise,"[68] the gift of salvation (see Rom. 6:23; 8:2; Phil. 2:16; 2 Cor. 2:16, etc.). When he therefore attributes "life" to

---

65. See pp. 91–97.

66. Wendt, *Begriffe*, pp. 146–47.

67. Ibid., p. 147.

68. Hermann Cremer, *Wörterbuch der neutestamentlichen Gräcität*, 5th ed. (Gotha, 1888), p. 393.

Christians in the present, then we will assume he has in mind not only ethical powers but also a life which, though still hidden beneath the veil of the earthly body, is nonetheless real and divine, a life which by its nature cannot fall prey to extinction.

Romans 6:4–8 above all supports this assumption. In contrast to Weiss,[69] Pfleiderer has preferred to construe the future ἐσόμεθα in verse 5, as well as the συζήσομεν in verse 8 of future, eternal life. Of course the future in verse 5 can also be construed as a logical future, but this seems out of the question in verse 8. If the καὶ συζήσομεν is intended to be the content of a conviction that follows logically from the ἀποθανεῖν σὺν Χριστῷ, then use of the term πιστεύειν for such a conviction is most surprising. In addition, according to verses 9–10 the συζῆν in verse 8 is conceived of as an immortal life. There would be nothing to indicate this, however, if συζήσομεν is a logical future. So it appears to me that Pfleiderer's view is definitely to be preferred. Weiss appears to be correct when he objects that συζήσομεν, "according to what precedes and follows (v. 11)," is "to be construed of ethical participation in the new and endless life of Christ." We concede, of course, that in essence the context speaks of the ethical life of Christians, to which, indeed, the problem raised in verse 1 gives witness. It appears to me that this difficulty can be resolved only in this way: For Paul, Christian existence within the new, pneumatic state, and the new moral life are not separate entities. Rather, the concept ζωή encompasses both. Thus in the same context the apostle can use ζωή in one instance to accent the moral life, and in the other the new state of existence. So also in Rom. 8:2 the νόμος τῆς ἁμαρτίας καὶ τοῦ θανάτου is contrasted with the νόμος τοῦ πνεύματος τῆς ζωῆς, that is, the law of two forces captive to sin and death is contrasted with the law of a life-creating power, and finally, sin and death are contrasted with life. So here too "life" denotes that which is opposed to sin as well as that which is opposed to death. The "new life" of Christians, therefore, just as the resurrection life of Jesus Christ in which they share (ὁμοίωμα τῆς ἀναστάσεως αὐτοῦ: 6:5), is to be understood not only as a new mode of conduct but also as a new form of existence. In precisely

---

69. See Weiss's *Römer* on the passage; idem, *Lehrbuch,* p. 333, n. 12; and Pfleiderer, *Paulinismus,* pp. 194–95.

the same way, Rom. 8:10—in which an ethical interpretation is prohibited by the context—makes no reference at all to a future possession, not even to its anticipation. Only in the final clause in verse 11 is there reference to a hope still awaited—the ζωοποίησις of our bodies. But the Spirit of the Christians is life already in the present, and there can be no more talk of its ζωοποίησις. "Thus our verse directly states the important thought that the ζωὴ αἰώνιος[70] is already present in Christian existence here and now, and above all as a still inward possession of the Spirit."[71]

Naturally, this fact is for Paul first of all a fact of faith, μὴ βλεπόμενον. But I doubt whether it is enough to speak merely of an "ideal possession of eternal life" or finally to conceive the present "life" of Christians as merely ethical.[72] Second Cor. 4:10 above all contradicts this view. There can be no doubt that the νέκρωσις τοῦ Ἰησοῦ in verse 10 and the εἰς θάνατον παραδίδοσθαι in verse 11 summarize what is described in verse 8 as θλίβεσθαι, ἀπορεῖσθει, and so on, namely, "the continual wearing away of his bodily existence through outward persecutions and physical illness."[73] But then we are forced to connect the verbs of the final clause in verses 10 and 11 with the οὐ στενοχωρεῖσθαι and so on of verses 8 and 9, that is, with the continual preservation of his bodily existence through the power of life in Jesus. This interpretation is supported above all by the fact that σῶμα, which is the subject here, can be exchanged for σάρξ (v. 11), an exchange which Pfleiderer's assumption that Paul is referring to the future resurrection of the body would not explain, since in the bodily resurrection the power of life in Jesus is not manifest in the σάρξ; it does not alter the natural fate of the σάρξ.[74] Thus, in the constant distresses that wear his body away Paul experiences the death of Jesus (see 1:9–10), but in the fact that despite all he does not die but rather

70. This expression is not quite accurate, since for Paul the ζωή always lies in the future; but in my opinion the subject is undoubtedly correct.

71. Pfleiderer, *Paulinismus,* p. 206.

72. Ibid., pp. 196ff. Gloël expresses himself more clearly on this point than does Pfleiderer (*Der heilige Geist,* pp. 188ff.), and totally agrees with us when he states that "in the present, however, the Christian possesses the life from God as an inward blessing."

73. Pfleiderer, *Paulinismus,* p. 204.

74. Contrary to ibid., p. 205.

retains his body, he sees at work in himself the power of Jesus and of Jesus' life. "It seems a wonder to him that in his weakness he is thus fit for work and exhibits an excess of power. For him, this is proof of the rule of Jesus' life, whose power to conquer death is manifest in his conduct and nature."[75] For the apostle, therefore, the assertion that he already possesses the ζωή Ἰησοῦ in the present is not an anticipation, a bold idea in which for an instant he is blissfully aware of already possessing what only the Parousia can really give. Rather, the possession of this ζωή Ἰησοῦ is for him a reality, the effect of which he may experience in himself daily! It is in direct analogy to 2 Cor. 4:7ff. when in 2 Cor. 13:3ff. Paul is confident of possessing "life with Christ by the power of God," a life to be demonstrated in his visit to the church as a dealing in power. Here, then, the ζωή σὺν Χριστῷ is to be referred to the demonstration of power in his apostleship. In exactly the same fashion "life" is also a being filled with moral energies to which moral conduct ought to correspond. Christians who have crucified the flesh and received new life in the Spirit so that they "live" or "are in the Spirit" (Gal. 5:25; Rom. 8:9) must also walk in the Spirit (Gal. 5:24–25). From the καινότης ζωῆς should follow an ἐν καινότητι ζωῆς περιπατεῖν (Rom. 6:4). "What is accomplished in principle is a task to be carried out in the particular."[76]

Paul more frequently describes this "life" as an object of Christian hope, and it is characteristic of him to regard the καινότης ζωῆς in Rom. 6:8, only a few verses after he had referred to it as a present possession (certainly in 6:4), as something hoped for. For Paul therefore "the life" is already present and yet is really still future; it is present but in the last analysis not yet quite realized. We are forced to see in this ambiguity of the concept a characteristic reproduction of the mood of the apostolic age, a mood that threads through the Pauline letters and had uncommonly great influence on the formation of the apostle's thought.[77] To give only one example, the same person is most intimately joined to Christ, so that Christ lives in

---

75. C.F. Georg Heinrici, *Das zweite Sendschreiben des Apostels Paulus an die Korinther* (Berlin, 1887), pp. 22–23; see also Lüdemann, *Anthropologie,* p. 145.

76. Ritschl, *Altkatholische Kirche,* p. 100.

77. See the further expositions in Ritschl, *Altkatholische Kirche,* pp. 96–97, in Pfleiderer, *Paulinismus,* pp. 225–26.

him and he in Christ; and the same person still feels separated from him as though by a barrier—ὅτι ἐνδημοῦντες ἐν τῷ σώματι ἐκδημοῦμεν ἀπὸ τοῦ κυρίου (2 Cor. 5:6). Here as well the same thing still delays the full realization of the pneumatic ζωή. To be sure, the Spirit is already life, but he is still present in a vessel that so little suits him; the Spirit that is life is still united with the fleshly body that is prey to death. The real organ of the Spirit, the pneumatic body, is not yet put on. The future life, as may be inferred from the Pauline analogies, will be related to the present as the ἀποκάλυψις (the term is from Rom. 8:19; see Col. 3:1-4) to the hidden possession. From this vantage point additional light falls on these expressions. The Christian is a καινή κτίσις (2 Cor. 5:17, etc.). The Creator God has begotten in him not only new conduct but also new life still hidden to the world!

In this speculation on ζωή—which, of course, is not widespread in Paul but nonetheless appears and forms the culmination of his utterances on the activities of the Spirit—the apostle summarizes everything he is able to derive from the Spirit: the new state of existence, the ethical powers, the charismata. The Christian has the πνεῦμα, which now means he has the ζωή, the blessing of salvation. With this idea Paul is farthest removed from the soil from which he sprang. There the Spirit was merely the power that works specific miracles and guarantees even greater ones; for Paul the present possession of the Spirit, τὸ πνεῦμα τῆς ζωῆς, is everything the Christian has for time and eternity. But we must emphasize that this statement, according to which the ζωή is already present, is not common in Paul. It was left to someone later, perhaps even greater, to set this Pauline idea at the midpoint of a system.

A PARALLEL IN THE TEACHING CONCERNING CHRIST

A noteworthy parallel to our apostle's teaching concerning the πνεῦμα is his doctrine of Christ. In other passages, all sorts of activities of the πνεῦμα appear as the activities of Christ himself. This is why in what was stated above we could occasionally use expressions concerning Christ to explain the teaching concerning the Spirit.

That hidden and pneumatic life which the apostle contends is already present is a growing together with Christ through the likeness of his resurrection life (Rom. 6:5). Future "eternal life" is life with or in Christ (Phil. 1:23; Rom. 6:8; 6:23); it is created through him, to be gained only in fellowship with him (Rom. 5:17–21; 1 Cor. 15:22; see also Rom. 8:2; 6:11)—it is Christ (Col. 3:4; Phil. 1:21). In Christ the person becomes a new creation (2 Cor. 5:17).

The apostle also derives his peculiar pneumatic endowment from Christ: his visions and revelations (2 Cor. 12:1) and his activity as an apostle (1 Cor. 3:5; Gal. 1:1). The apostle's authority over against the community rests on the life that he lives with Christ (2 Cor. 13:4). In the apostle's words it is Christ who speaks, and for this reason these words have power (2 Cor. 13:3). The coming together of the community and the apostle, which is referred to in 1 Cor. 5:4 and which levies a judgment on the incestuous person no human power could carry out, is a coming together in the power of the Lord Jesus. Through him Christ has wrought to win obedience from the Gentiles, by word and deed, by the power of signs and wonders (Rom. 15:18–19). The apostle is able to bring to the Romans the fullness of the blessing of Christ (Rom. 15:29). Christ is for him the power and the wisdom of God (1 Cor. 1:24). In him the apostle can do all things (Phil. 4:13).

Just as all the powers for moral and religious conduct can be derived from the Spirit, so they can be derived from Christ, and all the activities, moods, and experiences of the Christian can be set in relation to Christ. Christ is the life element in which the Christian exists. The Christians' calling and preservation, trust and hope, comfort and quickening, joy and peace, boast and victory, freedom and perfecting, death and life, love for God and the brethren—it is all "in Christ," "in the Lord."[78] The "fellowship" of Christ (1 Cor. 1:9) is that which binds all Christians together into one body (Rom. 12:5) and which annuls all differences that would otherwise separate them. Christ is all and in all! (Col. 3:11)

We must inquire how these statements concerning Christ are related to those concerning the Spirit. There is no doubt[79] that in some passages Paul alternates the two sequences of ideas in such fashion that he conceives the Spirit as proceeding from Christ. Christ's Spirit

---

78. Evidences in part from Pfleiderer, *Paulinismus,* p. 197.

79. Weiss, *Lehrbuch,* p. 328.

(Gal. 4:6; Rom. 8:9; 1 Cor. 2:16; 2 Cor. 3:17; Phil. 1:19) rules in the Christians. Christ works by the power of the Holy Spirit (Rom. 15:18–19). Whoever does not have the Spirit of Christ does not belong to him (Rom. 8:9). Christ is confessed by the Holy Spirit (1 Cor. 12:3). This conviction would thus express nothing essentially different from the corresponding early apostolic confession that Christ, the exalted one, has sent the Spirit down from heaven to believers.[80] Accordingly, the union of the individual Christian with Christ would not be direct but would be mediated through the Spirit; and we would only have to add to our description of Paul's teaching of the πνεῦμα that the Spirit is given to Christians through Christ. But it is still very much a question whether this statement plumbs the entire depth of the Pauline idea, and whether this explanation really does justice to everything the apostle has to say.

It must seem strange that in some passages Paul simply identifies the Spirit with Christ (1 Cor. 15:45; see 6:17; 2 Cor. 3:17). According to these passages the Spirit does not come through Christ; rather, Christ is himself this Spirit. This equation also appears when in one instance the Spirit is given in baptism (1 Cor. 12:13; 6:11) and in the other baptism is described as the beginning of most intimate union with the Lord (Rom. 6:3ff.; 1 Cor. 1:12–13; Gal. 3:27). Indeed, the entire parallel drawn above is evidence for the equation. In addition, the apostle does not weary of describing the peculiar relationship of Christians to their Lord in various figures. The Christian is alive in Christ (Rom. 6:11); Christ lives in him (Gal. 2:20); he is in Christ (Rom. 16:7; 8:1); Christ is in him (2 Cor. 13:5; Rom. 8:10); he is baptized into Christ (Rom. 6:3), crucified with him (Gal. 2:20, 6:14); he has endured his circumcision (Col. 2:11), has died with him (Col. 2:20, 3:3; Rom. 6:5–8), and has been buried with him (Rom. 6:4; Col. 2:12). He is raised with him (Rom. 6:5; Col. 3:1); he has put him on (Rom. 13:14; Gal. 3:27); he is united (κολλᾶσθαι) to him and thus becomes one spirit with him (1 Cor. 6:17). Christ is being formed in him (Gal. 4:19), and in "Christ" the believers are "filled" (Col. 2:10).

It must be admitted that these utterances describing the Christian's mysterious dying and rising in Christ "sound mystical."[81] If we think

80. See pp. 40–41.
81. See Weiss, *Lehrbuch*, p. 329.

we cannot accept their mystical interpretation, then we will have to regard all these words as inexact forms of expression. Thus, instead of ἐν Χριστῷ Paul should rather have written ἐν πνεύματι Χριστοῦ, and instead of Χριστὸς ἐν ἐμοί, he should have written πνεῦμα Χριστοῦ ἐν ἐμοί, and so on. But there can be no doubt that this interpretation of expressions that appear so often in Paul presents great difficulty. Are not the many figures Paul uses proof that for him life in fellowship with Christ is a mystery, impenetrable by human thought, indescribable in human words? In particular, the figure used of the sexual union in 1 Cor. 6:17 indicates how Paul conceives the incorporation of Christians in Christ—as a fellowship in which the person is absorbed in Christ and grows together with him so that both become "one spirit."

Second Cor. 4:11 especially speaks for the mystical interpretation. Jesus, who bears in himself the fullness of life, shares the power of his life with the apostle who is united to him so that it becomes manifest even in his mortal flesh. So also Jesus' suffering and death have become the apostle's own, and conversely, what Paul suffers he can call the παθήματα τοῦ Χιρστοῦ εἰς ἡμᾶς (see 2 Cor. 1:5; Col. 1:24).

It is easy to see how Paul came to this equation of πνεῦμα with Χριστός. Indeed, Paul's conversion did not occur through others' bringing him to faith in Jesus the Christ. The Lord himself appeared to him in his divine glory and seized him. Paul's first pneumatic experience was an experience of the Christ. From then on Christ was for him τὸ πνεῦμα. All the powers of the higher life which he may experience he derives from him; all the vicissitudes that he faces in his service he sets in relation to him—ἐμοὶ τὸ ζῆν Χριστός. But in order to understand Paul totally, we must consider one more thing: According to Paul, "Christ" is not a name for a principle. With this term he is always thinking of a person, of the one who showed his love in death, of the one on whom he calls, to whom he stands in a relation of prayer (2 Cor. 12:8–9), whom he loves (1 Cor. 16:22), and for whom he yearns (2 Cor. 5:6; Phil. 1:23). This gives the life of fellowship with Christ which Paul maintains its special coloration. For him Christ is more than the exalted Lord who already directs the destinies of his community and whose "slave" the Christian is. With all due reverence, Christ is also for him the beloved, to be in and with whom constitutes his joy and yearning in troubled hours. Paul's teaching concerning Christ is the expression of his deep and tender feeling, his thankful surrender to the one who had become his life. It is in this matter of the heart that his teaching concerning the πνεῦμα took on this peculiar shape.[82]

Accordingly, the teaching concerning the πνεῦμα and the teaching concerning Χριστός are parallel. What each has to say differs from the other merely by the fact that in the one the supernatural is derived from a divine power; in the other, it is derived from a divine person who has this power in himself. Neither teaching excludes the other, though either would have sufficed. It seems to me that the reason the teaching concerning the Χριστός, obviously more dear to the heart of Paul, did not suppress the teaching concerning the πνεῦμα is that Paul received his idea of the πνεῦμα with his education and continually witnessed it in his daily contact with the churches, and for that reason he naturally moved within a Jewish-Christian frame of thought. On the other hand, his teaching regarding the κοινωνία του Χριστοῦ is his original creation.

This explains why we cannot approve Pfleiderer's view as set forth in his *Paulinismus*.[83] The teaching regarding the πνεῦμα did not arise under the influence of Paul's teaching about Christ. Rather, the teaching about Christ is the peculiarly Pauline expression of what the apostle is contending for in his doctrine of the πνεῦμα which is borrowed from the views of the Christian community. This sequence in the two areas of his teaching is also supported by the fact that the formula ἐν Χριστῶ seems to be shaped after the analogy of the ἐν πνεύματι, also familiar to the primitive Christian community. In this expression the difference between Paul's view and the views of the community can easily be seen. For the community, ἐν πνεύματι denotes

---

82. But it would be a total misunderstanding of the apostle to construe this partial identification of Christ and τὸ πνεῦμα in such a way that Paul saw no activity of the exalted Christ which was not through the Spirit or as Spirit. Rather, the area of Christ's activity is greater than that of the Spirit. The former embraces much that is not an activity of the Spirit. Guiding the external destinies of believers toward the destruction of all their enemies is of course Christ's work; but he does not effect this through his Spirit, to whom such activity cannot be assigned. Christ's activity is thus not absorbed in the activity of his Spirit in the believers. This in contrast to frequent modernizations.

83. Pfleiderer, *Paulinismus,* pp. 202–3.

a being in ecstasy; for Paul, an existence in the life-begetting power of God. But the highest expression for his experience is ἐν Χριστῶ—in Christ.[84]

Naturally, I submit these statements with the reserve due any attempt at reconstruction which traces original lines.

---

84. Just as Paul, following popular opinion, conceived the reception of the Spirit as being mediated through faith and baptism, so he also fixed the beginning of fellowship with Christ in faith (Gal. 2:20) or in baptism. To examine how these two means relate to each other is not our task here. The question has also been raised as to whether Paul understood as the logically prior the reception of the Spirit or the fellowship with Christ. We will hardly insist that Paul answers this question, and it has no significance at all for him, since in both sequences of ideas he gives expression to the same experience, though in a different way. For him both are in juxtaposition; see Rom. 8, 9, 10; 2 Cor. 3:17, etc.

3
Related Concepts

Our intention up to now was to describe in broad outline Paul's teaching concerning the Spirit and to show how even though it sprang from the views of his age it still bears the stamp of the Pauline spirit. In order to secure our results from every aspect, we have yet to consider the relation between the concept of Spirit and those concepts often linked to it which explain or give a slight variation on the concept of the Spirit. We will thus give partial description of the place that this concept assumes within the whole of the Pauline teaching, but only insofar as it gives further explanation to the concept itself.[1]

SPIRIT AND THE HOLY

Paul very often uses πνεῦμα in some kind of connection with ἅγιος and its derivatives—in particular with the terms ἅγιον (twelve times, exclusive of the pastoral Epistles and the Epistle to the Ephesians) or ἁγιωσύνης (which occurs only in Rom. 1:4). But for Paul, as for later Christian dogmatics, the term ἅγιον is by no means a constant designation for the *"Spiritus Sanctus."* [2] More frequent in occurrence is τὸ πνεῦμα (thirty-three times) or πνεῦμα θεοῦ and related expressions (fourteen times), πνεῦμα Χριστοῦ (three times), and, in Paul, πνεῦμα

1. We do not regard it as our task to set forth the relationship between the concept of Spirit and such concepts as faith, word of God, community, atonement, justification, etc.; this differs from the treatment of Gloël.
2. In the synagogue the "designation 'Holy Spirit' was made a fixed concept" (J. Gloël, *Der heilige Geist in der Heilsverkündigung des Paulus* [Halle, 1888], p. 232). Even if this usage was already current prior to Paul, the way in which he knows and uses it but is by no means tied to it, in any event indicates that in his utterances concerning the Spirit the apostle repeats not the dogma of the synagogue but his own manifold world of experience (similarly ibid., p. 232).

without the article (twenty-five times).[3] It should be noted that in the later literature of Judaism ἅγιος is very often used as an *epitheton ornans* for divine things and persons.[4] Thus in the New Testament there is seldom any real difference in meaning between τὸ πνεῦμα or τὸ πνεῦμα τὸ ἅγιον. The narrative of Jesus' baptism in the synoptic Gospels, for example, is instructive in this regard. There we find descending on Jesus the πνεῦμα θεοῦ (Matt. 3:16), τὸ πνεῦμα (Mark 1:10), and τὸ πνεῦμα τὸ ἅγιον (Luke 3:22). And whether or not Paul gives the Spirit this designation seldom alters the sense. It is always the same divine power that he has in mind (see 1 Cor. 12:3, in which πνεῦμα θεοῦ alternates with πνεῦμα ἅγιον). We emphasize this because Issel[5] reckons almost solely with those Pauline utterances in which the word "*Holy* Spirit" happens to occur. By doing so he comes to the patently false conclusion that the Holy Spirit "is the consciousness of being favored by God,"[6] while he expressly excludes "the popular notion" that for Paul the Holy Spirit is "the impulse toward the good." This glaring fault which fully devaluates this portion of Issel's otherwise valuable writing is due to the false method he uses here. Instead of first establishing the concept of Spirit and then inquiring whether the epithet ἅγιος may add yet a nuance to the context in which it appears, he sets out immediately from the words *Holy Spirit*.

This nuance, as some scholars maintain, should be the relation to the Christian community. "The Spirit of God is called holy because he reveals himself within the elect and reconciled community of God."[7] This interpretation is clearly contradicted by such passages as Rom. 9:1 ("my conscience bears me witness in the Holy Spirit"); 2 Cor. 6:6, in which Paul names the Holy Spirit in addition to all the Christian virtues, and, indeed, as their principle; and by 1 Thess. 1:5, in which the apostle states that he preached the gospel not only in word but also

---

3. This generally occurs where there is reference to the concept of the Spirit as such, that is, where the Spirit is to be described according to his nature as "spirit" (see ibid., p. 387).

4. See Ernst Issel, *Der Begriff der Heiligkeit im Neuen Testament* (Leiden, 1887), p. 48.

5. Ibid., pp. 53ff.

6. Ibid., p. 56.

7. H.H. Wendt, *Die Begriffe Fleisch und Geist* (Gotha, 1878), p. 53; similarly Hermann Cremer, *Wörterbuch der neutestamentlichen Gräcität,* 5th ed. (Gotha, 1888), e.g., pp. 51, 741ff.

in power and in the Holy Spirit and with full conviction. Where is there in these passages any relation to the "elect and reconciled community of God"? Since agreement has not yet been reached in a similar dispute regarding קדוש in the Old Testament, we can only state here that we approve of the statements of Schultz:[8] God is holy, that is, "God is the one incomparably exalted above the world, who preserves his majesty removed from all dishonor. . . . Everything that is his possession shares in this majesty and requires the same reverence." Accordingly, the Spirit in the New Testament is called holy because, belonging to God, he shares in the divine majesty and inviolability and must thus be treated with reverential awe.[9] For this reason in Mark 3:29, Acts 5:3, 7:51, Eph. 4:30, Heb. 6:4, and 1 Thess. 4:8 (in the Old Testament, in Isa. 63:10) the Spirit is called "holy" in order to show the severity of the sin against him. For whoever offends against the Spirit by speaking blasphemously of him, lying to him, resisting him, grieving him, despising him, sins against that which is holy, against that which belongs to the divine majesty and is inviolable. All the more fearsome must be the judgment meted out to such an offender. From the prophetic period and on, the divine holiness is thought of chiefly as the "majesty of a moral God who governs the world,"[10] "as the purity which abhors all sin."[11] And that which is opposed to the holy, the profane, is also that which is sinful. Thus when Paul speaks in Rom. 9:1 of his conscience bearing him witness in the Holy Spirit, he has in mind that the Spirit, because he is holy, is absolutely removed from all sin, does not allow a lie. The addition of ἁγίῳ thus serves to confirm the truth of this witness of conscience in the Spirit. Now, whomever the Holy Spirit takes into possession by that fact becomes himself holy (see 1 Cor. 3:16–17); he is

8. Hermann Schultz, *Alttestamentliche Theologie,* 2d ed. (Frankfurt am Main, 1878), p. 517.

9. "Holy" never *denotes* the same as "belonging to God" or "God's possession" but means only pertaining to God's majesty, unapproachable and inviolable. Holiness is thus an attribute of every divine possession, and one may conclude that if something is called holy it belongs to God. But "holy" is not identical to "belonging to God." This contrary to frequent misinterpretations, also in Gloël, *Der heilige Geist,* pp. 233–34.

10. Schultz, *Alttestamentliche Theologie,* p. 519.

11. Issel, *Heiligkeit,* p. 26.

sanctified by the Holy Spirit (Rom. 15:16; 1 Cor. 6:11; see 2 Thess. 2:13; 1 Cor. 1:2,30).[12] For through the indwelling of the Spirit the person has become God's temple, a holy temple. This means first of all that the person who has the Holy Spirit and has thus become God's possession and no longer belongs to himself (1 Cor. 6:19) for this very reason shares in God's inviolable majesty. The one filled with the Spirit is a sanctuary, inviolable, unassailable for himself and for others. For εἴτις τόν ναὸν τοῦ θεοῦ φθείρει, φθερεῖ τοῦτον ὁ θεός! (1 Cor. 3:17). In Paul's hands this idea is an uncommonly effective argument when he must admonish to "sanctification," that is, to deeming what is holy as holy. Whoever, as, for example, in 1 Cor. 6:18ff., sins against his body through whoredom sins against the temple of the Holy Spirit: φθερεῖ τοῦτον ὁ θεός! This makes it obvious that the life the Holy Spirit begins within the person is a holy life, pure and free from all sin. Through baptism, in which the Spirit is given, persons allow themselves to be washed. They are sanctified and justified (1 Cor. 6:11), and the ἡγιάσθητε "denotes not merely dedication to kinship with God, but in principle a moral purification and sanctification."[13] Then, of course, it is also the Holy Spirit who more and more brings the Christian to a state of holiness in terms of separation from all sins, that is, to a state of moral purity. For Paul, therefore, to be pleasing to God and to be sanctified by the Holy Spirit is one and the same (Rom. 15:16). In this sense, to be sanctified by the Spirit is the goal of the Christian life (γένηται!). When consciousness of the love of God (Rom. 5:5), the Christian's joy in believing (Rom. 14:17 and 1 Thess. 1:6), the Christian's hope (Rom. 15:13), an ecstatic confession (1 Cor. 12:3), all Christian virtues (2 Cor. 6:6), and the bold preaching of Paul (1 Thess. 1:5) are all derived from the Holy Spirit, and when the Spirit in whom all Christians are to share is called holy (2 Cor. 13:13), then the epithet "holy" is to be regarded merely as an *epitheton ornans* that is superfluous in the context and expresses the apostle's reverence for the Spirit, the gift of God.

In accord with the spirited tone of the introduction to Romans, the

---

12. Thus, according to Paul, the Spirit is not holy because he belongs to the community; rather, the community is holy because it is given the Spirit.

13. Otto Pfleiderer, *Paulinismus* (Leipzig, 1873), p. 212.

πνεῦμα ἁγιωσύνης in 1:4 is a Hebrew parallel for πνεῦμα ἅγιον (πνεῦμα ἁγιασμοῦ and πνεῦμα ἁγιωσύνης in Testament of Levi 18). Actually both expressions, "a Spirit to whom holiness belongs" (the genitive of quality) and "a Spirit who is holy," are altogether identical—as proved from the parallels in The Testaments of the Twelve Patriarchs. For this reason, we are suspicious of explaining this choice of terms on other then rhetorical grounds as does Weiss,[14] who states that Paul intended to distinguish "the Spirit originally in Christ from the Spirit given through him." Yet we agree with Weiss that Paul expressly accents the holiness of the Spirit in Christ in order to allow that "natural state" to appear "which qualified Christ for the exaltation predicated of him here." For according to that aspect of his nature by which he possessed the spirit of holiness, Christ was unassailable, under the divine protection, and for this reason death could not hold him (Acts 2:24).

SPIRIT AND FREEDOM

Of greater significance for the concept of the Spirit is the relation of the Spirit to the concept of freedom. In 2 Cor. 3:17 is enunciated the fundamental principle that οὗ τὸ πνεῦμα κυρίου, ἐλευθερία! The confidence with which Paul introduces this sentence without proof clearly indicates that from the nature of the Spirit the freedom of the one inspired must necessarily follow. In exactly the same way, Gal. 5:18 states the axiom that εἰ πνεύματι ἄγεσθε, οὐκ ἐστὲ ὑπὸ νόμον. That the purpose of verses 19–23 is not to prove this statement is clear from the fact that verse 19 is not linked to verse 18 by the γάρ but rather by the δέ. Now, this connection of Spirit and freedom is uncommonly characteristic. Since the Spirit is a power who because of his supernatural origin is absolutely superior to every natural power, and also towers in strength above whatever else is supernatural (demons, the Law, etc.), so he bears his law solely in himself. The Spirit is as the wind that blows where it wills (John 3:8). No power on earth may summon him. He is his own master. Thus, wherever the Spirit is, there

---

14. Bernhard Weiss, *Lehrbuch der biblischen Theologie des Neuen Testaments,* 4th ed. (Berlin, 1884), p. 291.

is freedom. Whoever is in the service of a higher Lord, no one can command.

> Who may order me to halt? Who dictate to
> the spirit leading me? The arrow must
> fly whither the hand of its archer sends it.[15]

These words, placed by the poet in the mouth of his heroine, correspond totally to the New Testament concept of the Spirit— she is bound by the Spirit from within but conscious that for this very reason she is free from every external command. Whomever the Spirit rules is by that fact raised above every other law. This thought in Gal. 5:18 is an argument for the fact that Christians can no longer be under the Mosaic law.[16] The greater power of the Spirit has freed them from the lesser power of the Law. Further, wherever the Spirit of life holds sway, there flesh, sin, and death have no power (e.g., Rom. 8:2; see 6:22). "Thus, according to Rom. 8:2, deliverance from the law of sin and death grounded in Christ Jesus follows from the truth that a superior law, the law of the Spirit, opposed it."[17] Πνεῦμα and ἐλευθερία are thus correlative, as are πνεῦμα and ζωή. From these clues regarding the freedom of the Spirit-bearer, a passage such as 1 Cor. 14:38 (εἰ δέ τις ἀγνοεῖ, ἀγνοείτω) becomes clear. Paul thinks it possible that the prophets will appeal his instructions to the superior power of the Spirit who is at work in them in a fashion he does not desire. He knows full well that there is no higher court against such an appeal. The Spirit is free. Of course, the apostle contends he also has the Spirit and speaks in the name of the Lord (v. 37), and anyone who ignores this does so at his peril. Paul must content himself with having spoken the truth. Whether one follows him is another question. In such matters commands cannot be given. Thus the same autonomy

15. Friedrich Schiller, "Jungfrau von Orleans," 2:4. In many of its details, the description of the maid by our ingenious poet corresponds (indeed, apart from its one chief point, namely, the law which the mother of God imposes on her) to the portrait we must draw for ourselves of a New Testament prophet. To understand the New Testament it is not a thankless task to study prophecy in light of the figure sketched by the poet.

16. See also Gal. 4:23ff. in Gloël, *Der heilige Geist,* p. 265.

17. Gloël, *Der heilige Geist,* p. 271.

that Paul claims for his apostleship—an apostleship not from men but from God—and in face of every attack, he also assumes in thoroughgoing fashion for all other pneumatics. So the reading ἀγνοείτω is not to be rated less than the ἀγνοεῖται for reasons of sense.[18] Generally, a basic feature of Paul's letters is that he treats all the Christian communities as independent entities. Christians are free men of the Spirit whom one admonishes but does not command. This is a practical consequence of Paul's teaching concerning the freedom of the pneumatic, a teaching which, of course, has quite different consequences for the individual Christian life and which represents "no less a high point in the history of morality" than does "justification by faith in the history of religion."[19] But further discussion does not belong here. We were concerned merely with the connection of the two concepts, Spirit and freedom.[20]

SPIRIT AND FLESH (MATTER)

We have yet to deal with the relationship between the concepts πνεῦμα and σάρξ. Since the studies by Holsten this question has continually drawn the attention of biblical scholars, and there is considerable literature concerned with it.

Despite this fact we cannot say that the question has been answered, much less that any agreement has been reached to date. There is still considerable difference of opinion on the chief question of the relation between the two concepts σάρξ and ἁμαρτία in Paul. And I do not believe that we can discuss this question even at the present time. What is lacking, above all, is a thorough investigation of the anthropology of the Old Testament, and the anthropology of Palestinian Judaism is, up to now, all but fallow ground. Pfleiderer,[21] of course, has noted the similarity between the rabbinic and Pauline an-

---

18. Contrary to F. Georg Heinrici on the passage, *Das erste Sendschreiben des Apostels Paulus an die Korinther* (Berlin, 1880), p. 462, n. 1.

19. Pfleiderer, *Paulinismus,* p. 22.

20. Gloël gives a detailed discussion of the relation between the two concepts (*Der heilige Geist,* pp. 256–70), but he does not too clearly and lucidly describe the necessary and direct connection between the two concepts, as set forth above.

21. Otto Pfleiderer, *Urchristentum* (Berlin, 1887), pp. 163ff., 187.

thropology, and Gloël[22] has followed suit. But it is still not proper to use the material compiled in Weber[23] as a source for pre-Pauline views. Since the question of Jewish views has not yet been answered, we have no firm ground beneath our feet for the Pauline anthropology. This much can be assumed from the very outset: If Paul is anywhere in harmony with contemporary ideas, then it is in his anthropological expression and views. But the prior question with respect to this area in Pauline theology is: Did the pessimistic mood that prevailed in Hellenistic Judaism at the time of Christ (according to which man's sensuousness, the body of flesh which ties him to this world of sense, is the real and final cause of his sinfulness) also find entry with Palestinian Judaism? The apocalypses would yield special material here. Their thought, directed toward the end time and congenial to the eschatological tendency in Paul, may have fostered the penetration of pessimistic moods. On the other hand, a final answer to our question with respect to Paul would be possible only if we treated in detail Paul's ethical views, where, of course, the consequences of his anthropology will everywhere be found.

For these reasons, then, I will dispense with any further indication of the relation between σάρξ and πνεῦμα and deal only with the question for which we compiled the Jewish material above: Does Paul conceive the πνεῦμα as being in some sense material? From our remarks[24] we might assume so. Paul, however, was educated in dialectics. We may assume he was able to conceive of ideas in purely abstract fashion without at the same time visualizing them. So nothing can be stated a priori. To employ the use of language as proof for the materiality of the Spirit[25] is a highly doubtful practice. It is obvious that Paul had to appropriate the usage available to him. What other expressions should he use? The metaphor in 2 Cor. 4:6, used for the sake of an allusion to Gen. 1:3, proves just as little. On the other

---

22. Gloël, *Der heilige Geist,* p. 246, n. 1.

23. Ferdinand Weber, *System der altsynagogalen palästinensischen Theologie* (Leipzig, 1880).

24. Above, pp. 59–66.

25. Carl Holsten, *Zum Evangelium des Paulus und des Petrus* (Rostock, 1868), p. 378; Pfleiderer, *Paulinismus,* p. 201.

hand, the Spirit is clearly linked to a heavenly substance (1 Cor. 15:44, σῶμα πνευματικόν). Here, I must confess I do not understand how these words could be translated "a body formed from the substance of the πνεῦμα."[26] Quite apart from the wider context of the passage, it is impossible to translate σῶμα ψυχικόν differently from σῶμα πνευμα-τικόν. If the former is not a body formed from the ψυχή but rather a body that corresponds to the nature of ψυχή and is its natural medium,[27] how can σῶμα πνευματικόν be anything but a σῶμα that by nature corresponds to the πνεῦμα and is thus suited to be the perfect means of its manifestation?[28] Thus, in the phrase σῶμα πνευματικόν nothing is said of the substance of the body.[29] Certainly! But it is just as certain that these terms assume that the future heavenly, spiritual body will not again consist of earthly flesh and that for this reason the Spirit has its appropriate vehicle not in the body of flesh related to the soul but rather in a body formed from another, heavenly substance. This means that a quite discreet and transcendent substance is intimately connected with the Spirit. Paul himself makes clear in 1 Cor. 15:43 that we are to conceive this transcendent body as intransitory, glorious, and mighty.[30] Second Cor. 3:18 presents a special difficulty. We do not think it is possible to interpret the idea of the μετα-μορφοῦσθαι ἀπὸ δόξης εἰς δόξαν beyond any question. Within the total context, the word δόξα denotes the sublimity and glory of a person or institution, or also the splendor proceeding from God or Christ and reflected by whomever he illumines. It is precisely the same as with the Old Testament term כבוד. We may not insist that Paul himself would not have approved the second notion, that is, the sensuous and naive view of the divine כבוד. Paul was no child of the Enlightenment.[31] On this ambiguity of the term rests the entire context

26. Pfleiderer, *Paulinismus,* p. 201, assumes this translation.

27. See Holsten, *Zum Evangelium,* p. 375; Weiss, *Lehrbuch,* p. 241, n. 8.

28. Gloël, *Der heilige Geist,* p. 366.

29. Ibid.

30. See Weiss, *Lehrbuch,* pp. 283–84.

31. But many modern exegetes are wont to prove their origin from the Enlightenment by their total inability to come to terms with such naive views. They prefer to exclude them outright. Of course, these errors could only arise by the usual method of viewing the New Testament in isolation and not in connection with Judaism and the apostolic age.

in which the splendor appearing on Moses' face at the giving of the Law occurs for the sake of glorifying his mediatorial function. This allegorical play on a word with a dual meaning is quite according to the taste of the rabbinic מדרש, for that is what is occurring here. If the δόξα κυρίου in verse 18 denotes the glory of the exalted one, then the δόξα given those who behold him is the glory of the Christians' inner, moral life in which they share more and more. The other interpretation is just as probable, namely, that the glory is also thought of as a luminous, heavenly splendor. The idea then would be that by beholding Christ, believers receive an ever greater heavenly splendor, a splendor, we may add, still ἐν μυστηρίῳ, but some day, at the Parousia, shining forth in all its light. The fact that Paul seldom makes use of this idea but always reserves the "transfiguration" for the future proves nothing against this interpretation—still less, since we have analogies in the concepts ζωή, σωτηρία, and δικαιοσύνη. And incidentally, in that great fragment we call the Pauline theology there is many an ἅπαξ λεγόμενον. A sober exegesis will not object that this interpretation resists modern thought. Modern theology has simply stripped away the naive concept of the δόξα (splendor). The context does not render a decision on the two interpretations, so we must keep the question open. Naturally, our inability to interpret 2 Cor. 3:18 with any certainty does not at all impair the results that we obtained in the other way. This idea that the Spirit is linked to a heavenly substance is by no means specifically Pauline, nor is it specifically Christian; it is of Jewish origin. We indicated a parallel to 1 Corinthians 15 in The Apocalypse of Baruch, chapter 51.[32] Further, we should note here that for Paul the Spirit is first of all a transcendent power. The suggestion that it is linked to a heavenly substance is a δευτέρα φροντίς. This must be observed in any description of the Pauline teaching concerning the πνεῦμα. So we cannot at all approve of making the substantiality of the Spirit a point of departure in the description of this teaching,[33] though it is altogether appropriate for Gloël to treat this question only in last place.[34]

32. See pp. 62–63.
33. This is what occurs in Holsten *(Zum Evangelium)*, Lüdemann *(Anthropologie)*, and Pfleiderer *(Paulinismus)*.
34. Gloël, *Der heilige Geist,* pp. 372ff.

THE INFLUENCE OF THE PAULINE TEACHING
CONCERNING THE SPIRIT

Paul's teaching concerning the πνεῦμα had very great influence in the period following, in any event, an influence greater than his teaching regarding justification. While the latter had to remain intelligible to Gentile Christians, his teaching concerning the πνεῦμα was intelligible wherever there were "pneumatic" phenomena. All the post-Pauline writings witness to the epoch-making significance of this very teaching—the writings of the New Testament as well as those of the apostolic fathers. The theology of the Gospel of John clearly indicates its dependence on Paul on this subject. In our time, what remains of the pneumatic appearances of the apostolic age is merely the doctrine of the inspiration of the New Testament Scriptures, shaped in a time when "the Spirit was no longer in Israel." In the Catholic church, the concept of office was added to it.[35] From Paul we have a more valuable bequest. "Come, Holy Ghost" is still sung on his terms. Indeed, just as only the person who is able or desires to think himself into the supernatural world view can understand Paul's teaching concerning the πνεῦμα, so only the person who approves of this world view can teach concerning the Spirit in the full New Testament sense of the term, that is, in the Pauline sense.

35. See Adolf von Harnack, *Lehrbuch der Dogmengeschichte,* 2d ed. (Freiburg im Breisgau, 1888), 1:366–67.

Index of
Passages Cited